LOAN SHARKS

THE RISE AND RISE OF
PAYDAY LENDING

ISBN: 978-1-907720-98-7

Typeset and designed by Deirdré Gyenes

LOAN SHARKS

THE RISE AND RISE OF
PAYDAY LENDING

By Carl Packman

Searching finance

About the author
CARL PACKMAN is a writer, researcher, and blogger. He has written for many publications including the Guardian, New Statesman, American Banker, Jewish Chronicle and Credit Today Magazine. He regularly appears on the BBC, Sky News, LBC Radio and Channel 4 to talk about issues surrounding problem debt and the payday lending industry. Packman has worked with various organisations including Compass, the Centre for Labour and Social Studies and the Trades Union Congress on publications dealing with the welfare state, debt, and the shadow banking industry. He lives in London.

About Searching Finance
Searching Finance publishes and curates economics, finance and politics. Follow us on Facebook at www.facebook.com/searchingfinance.
Our website is: www.searchingfinance.com

CONTENTS

ACKNOWLEDGEMENTS

THERE ARE too many people I could thank, and inevitably I will forget someone, but I want to start by giving my sincerest thanks to those who allowed me to interview them. In no particular order, thank you to Stewart Lansley, John Moorwood, Sean O'Connel, John Paul David, Mick McAteer, Damon Gibbons, Tim Worstall, Francis Coulson, Sara Brooks, Gillian Guy, Rod McKee, Yvonne Fovargue MP, Nic Daikin MP, Damian Hinds MP, Elaine Kempson, Chris Dillow, Veronika Thiel, Matthew Fulton, Helen Goodman MP, Tracey Crouch MP, Legal Bizzle, Faisel Rahman, Chris Cook, Wes Streeting, Stella Creasy MP, Ian Murray MP, Margot Finn, John Spriggs, Dr Ruth Cherrington, Andrew Percy MP, Sally Chicken, Jackie Doyle-Price, Sarah-Jane Lynch, David Schurjin, Dr Richard Wellings, Steve Perry, Una Farrell, Saloman Raydan Rivas, John Gathergood, Larry Elliot, Left Outside, Paul Crayston, Fiona Hoyle, Gerard Brody, Gavin Anderson, David Rodger, Russell Hamblin-Boone, Carol Highton, Marc Gander, Emma Bryn-Jones, Alan Whitehead MP, Michael Thomas, Andrew Percy MP, Cllr Shona Johnstone, Kevin Waters, Keith Dryburgh, and Derek Twigg MP.

I would also like to thank those individuals who have allowed me to put relevant written work on their publications, during the period that I have been writing this book. They are, in no order: Sunny Hundal, Shamik Das, Alex Hern, Dr Eoin Clarke and Jon Lansman. I must also thank the two people with whom I share a blog: Paul Cotterill and Dave Semple. Furthermore, I should like to give my thanks to the following individuals for the help they gave me to get to MPs, people in the industry, tips and just for general conversations regarding the subject, which have proved extremely helpful: Gareth Gould, Pauline Baker, Dr Phil Burton Cartledge, Michael Ezra, Jonathan Botten, Andrew Barret, Ed Smith (for his best efforts), Max Wind-Cowie, Beatriz Iglesias Tolosa, Rowenna Davis, Miljenko Williams, Jake Sumner, Katherine O'Brien, Jill Hume, Will Black, Simon Gompertz, Andrew Lownie, Michael O'Connell and Zahrah Mostaque.

I give special thanks to Ashwin Rattan and the team at Searching Finance for publishing this work. From the time I first met Ashwin in the Bree Louise pub in Euston, until the present day, he has always been very supportive of the work I have been doing and very helpful in introducing me to relevant and important people.

Finally, I want to thank my parents, Keith and Sharon Packman, who have both been an incredible source of support, and whose love and affection has always motivated me to work hard and push myself. Without them, I would not be where I am today.

PREFACE

Before the original publication of my book *Loan Sharks* I heard some very well meaning criticisms of my work, along the lines of the following: *we realise that payday lending is bad but it is only a symptom, not a cause, of the economic crisis– therefore should we not focus our attention on taking down the whole system which has allowed this type of industry to proliferate?*

Indeed agitator and l'enfant terrible Brendan O'Neill said in a column in September 2013[i] that: "a socialism which obsesses over a symptom of the economic downturn rather than putting forward ideas for how to create a new and wealthy society is ... pretty foolish." Strictly speaking, of course, I'm not against looking at global problems and how to pursue ideas and actions that counter their growth. I do think that Wonga.com and the like exist in a system that has ultimately predicated itself along the premises that if you leave the market to control itself then all will eventually come to profit from its genius. At best capitalism is the worst existing system to run things... apart from all the other ones.

How I would add to this, is by saying that the local informs the national, which in turn informs the global, and vice versa. I do absolutely believe that we start at the local. For example we know what happened in the lead up to the financial crisis. Regulators (when the word regulation is a bad one even for regulators themselves you know you're in trouble; and who was watching over the federal reserve on the eve of the crash?

Alan Greenspan, student of Ayn Rand, the Queen of quasi Darwinian, anti-state market fundamentalism) kept their eyes off the game, got greedy, and now economies the world over suffer. But how often do we hear about the personal debt crises that happen on a daily basis? What about the working class household who work all the hours god sends only to fall behind on a bill payment when the fridge breaks and are left to miss meals? Or the single mother who is trying to work out whether it will pay for her to work or not? Or the labourer who can't make it to the end of the month on his wages alone, who walks down his high road only to be bombarded with messages about easy cash, money in minutes, payday come early? Or the family with children who have realised that they need at least £24,000 a year to afford the basics[ii]? When times are tough for these people what news stories do we see? Any on them and their plight? Not likely. Will they be bailed out like the banks were? Absolutely not.

So why payday lending?

In 2014 consumer credit might still mostly be sold to consumers by mainstream banks but that is only for now. Since 1989 7,500 mainstream banks and building societies have closed and they have been closing 3.5 times faster in traditional manufacturing and inner city areas than in suburban ones[iii]. So is this all down to online banking or nobody wanting to go to a branch anymore? The numbers don't stack up. Banks are withdrawing themselves from certain areas and denying basic products to a lot more people. Whether this is by design or through competition is disputable. As I point out elsewhere in this book PwC, in their 2012 report Precious Plastic[iv], pointed out that credit cards were going through a mid-life crisis. And while plastic grew frail and old who were one of the winners? Why, the payday lending industry of course.

In just 9 years the industry has grown from being worth £100m (in 2004) to a bloated £2.2bn in 2013. The National Debtline recorded 465 calls in 2007 on payday lending for the whole year, now they receive up to 100 per day. The debt charity StepChange recorded 36,000 calls made to it in 2012, twice the number in 2011 – and that is on course to double again for 2013. A survey of Unite members looking at how many of their members resorted to payday loans found that the average amount taken out over a month was £200 in March 2012. To show how bad things became in that one year come September the figure had shot up to £328. By August 2013 the average amount members were taking out with expensive, high cost, short term credit lenders online or on the high street was a massive £660. Paying that back, with interest, would not be a short term affair for anyone.

This is all big business now. Nine out of the leading 10 payday lenders in the UK doubled their profits from 2011 to 2012. One of the biggest, Wonga, made £63m, over £1m per week. While real incomes fall to below 2003 levels, the cost of living rises, food prices rise above wages; debt is a solid cash cow for the payday industry. They can't believe their luck.

So while I don't dismiss the national issues, and the global issues, I do most definitely see the local issues as key to taking action on inequality and crisis. The financial crisis will be resolved in time, but what matters as much is curbing the personal debt crisis. Household debt is rising, and it is rising all the more as the mainstream withdraws itself and leaves people to the mercy of the fringe. Consumer credit is one such example. Mainstream banks shut shop and payday lenders prey on the poor. Their profit margins go up, there's less money in the pockets of the many, consumer-led growth is a pipe dream designed only to make people like Chancellor George Osborne sound optimistic and compassionate.

Fortunately payday lending has a bad image now. And unsurprisingly so. If you'd asked me a few years ago what makes people and the press outraged about the industry I would have said primarily the interest rates. Once upon a time, whenever you read an article or talked to someone in the street about The Money Shop or Wonga they would usually cite the interest rates that stray well into 4,000 per cent (with Wonga it is 5,000 per cent). But as time has gone on the general criticism has developed. We can all see that annualised percentage ratings are an inaccurate measure. Martin Lewis, the money saving expert who has spent a lot of time denigrating the industry, amusingly put it this way: "I did a pet calculation the other day which showed that if I lent you £20 and said, 'Pay me back a pint of beer next week; buy me a pint for it,' and the pint cost £3, that's 141,000% interest, if you compound it. Yet most people would say, 'Buy me a pint and £20, is a pretty reasonable deal.'"

Most are agreed that APR is confusing and that a system where prices were publicised in pounds and pence would be far simpler. But there is still outrage against the payday lenders. Why is that? In brief it is because in March 2013 in the lead up to the Office of Fair Trading notifying lenders that they were under a full investigation for widespread failure to comply with regulation and guidance, it was spelt out in plain language what kind of bad practices the industry was up to. This could not have been any plainer when Citizens Advice called for action on payday lenders after they'd received information about them lending to people who were under-18, who had mental health difficulties, and who were drunk. Furthermore, and simply put, it is because these companies make huge profits while the loans they sell are extremely expensive. To take a loan out, on average, of £200 for 14 days with a high street lender could cost you in interest payments around £50. That is not cheap. With an online lender taking out the same amount it could be up to £70 for charges. And this doesn't include late fees or add-ons if that principal loan was rolled over. This is what Stella Creasy MP told me was the poverty premium that many people faced.

But what if people didn't have the likes of Wonga?

The question is very frequently asked: *if we didn't have Wonga and other companies like them wouldn't it just be the case that people live on the streets or approach baseball bat wielding loan sharks on sink estates?* The answer, however, is simple. This is what payday lenders say to clear their consciences. The Office of Fair Trading have shown that payday lenders are reckless themselves. They lend when they shouldn't, to people who will inevitably suffer more financial hardship if they continue payments on a credit product that clearly wasn't appropriate for them in the first place. There are places where these consumers can go, where they can receive the sort of financial advice they deserve, where they can be placed on debt repayment plans that will take into consideration their monthly outgoings in a way that is not pressuring them to take out more expensive loans, and where they can borrow at affordable rates. If payday lenders were responsible lenders they would signpost credit unions to many of those who approach them. Given the data shown by the OFT and Citizens Advice we can see that a great many people who take out loans regret the decision afterwards. Take for example Wonga, who boast their "high" customer satisfaction rates. YouGov surveyed some of its borrowers in 2013 and found that the company scored worse than Ryanair for satisfaction. Interviewing 89 borrowers at random 24 per cent were satisfied, 41 per cent dissatisfied, and 35 per cent neutral.[v]

Payday lenders if they were responsible would forego profit maximisation and refer more people to the services of credit unions rather than put people into potentially medium and long term debt cycles, which is a common occurrence with payday loans. But at the moment they do not do so. A credit union is far more likely to have a referral from the illegal moneylending teams than by a payday lender who comes to figure that a potential customer would realise a far greater amount of financial hardship if they continued with the transaction.

What is more likely, and the reason the whole industry was placed under investigation by the OFT in the first place, is that payday lenders want more money. A comic strip in Viz Magazine in 2013 depicted a branch manager of a made up shop called MEGAMONEYMARKET. A tense looking man approaches the manager and requests a loan of £150. Simple enough. The manager requests in return that the man sign all the forms he has prepared "and the £200 will be in your account later today". Confused, the tense man, now even more tense than ever, notes that he only requested £150, to which the manager replies "*Whoops!* Was probably on my mind that the arrangement fees are the same for *any* loan *up* to £200, an *amazing* deal!" The point here being that payday lenders are financially incentivised to lend more, trap the individual in debt, and hope that when at the end of the month they need another loan to service that original one they come back. These companies can make, remember, up to £1m a week. Debt is a growth industry! And I bet you didn't realise Viz was so educational.

Or take for example the regional manager of Cheque Centre in Scotland who told workers in an email "not to offer simple, fixed repayment plans to people struggling to pay back loans with crippling interest rates."[vi] Keeping people in debt was what made all the money – if the regulators were flimsy on regulating, what incentive was there for the Cheque Centre to do anything else? Compassion? Wrong industry.

When we entertain the "what if, what if" argument from payday lenders we effectively say that poor people must put up or shut up. I spoke to a woman about her payday loan debts and she told me she was thinking about getting a new phone because after taking one out, and eventually paying it off, she would still receive tens of emails daily offering new and cheap loans. When the loans company First Financial were rapped for sending texts to people with the message "Hi Mate I'm still out in town, just got £1000 in my account from these guys www.firstpaydayloanuk.co.uk"[vii] it was not a one off – similar text messages come through thick and fast for some people, whether they've taken out loans or not sometimes. You'd forget sometimes that there are existing harassment laws for such things.

We can't blame payday lenders for the global crisis that has seen banks withdraw themselves, but we can blame them for what they do. And their behaviour has, time and time again, been shown to have no regard for either the law nor the finances of its borrowers. So when they say things could be worse without them, they ignore that things are bad as they are. Forget this race to the bottom, people deserve better. The law even permits that, with the OFT dedicating hundreds of pages of guidelines for responsible lending. But a mixture of profit motivation from lenders and thumb twiddling from the regulator has meant a poor deal is the only option for some.

Payday rebranding

There was a very brief, but ultimately pointless, attempt to rebrand. While some chief executives of payday lenders continued their silence, some became more vocal. Wonga continued to tell the press that it wasn't a payday lender as people could pay back their loans any time they wanted (forgetting that this was not what marks out a payday lender). One company, Pounds2Pocket, the trading name of a company called CashEuroNet UK which was under investigation by the Office Fair Trading, even went as far as offering a unique product, unlike any other of the payday type loans.

The 12 month loan was the new frontier. Much like personal loans from more mainstream providers this was going to be living proof that not only was a short term product that banks didn't offer in high demand, but payday lenders could actually take on the likes of Barclays and HSBC on their own turf. If you hadn't heard about it then that's probably the main point

– it wasn't the success story they were hoping for. The rates of interest (which really do matter in this instance because APR, as an annualised calculation, over 12 months, does give you an indication of what you'll be paying back) of up to 278 per cent – meaning that repayments will already be over twice the amount you have borrowed, excluding fees and penalties that might be incurred (Pounds to Pocket, for example, charge £12 for their penalty fees) – are enough to put anyone off.

On the Pounds2Pocket website it said that as a first time borrower up to £2000 can be applied for. It gave a representative example of £449.01 charged in interest on a loan of £500, meaning the total paid back for a loan of £500 is £949.01. This is exclusive of other administrative fees. This price, as it stated on the website, is based on a fixed interest rate of 140% APR and is subject to "strict lending criteria", which if a potential customer doesn't meet then they could be offered an "alternative product with different terms". If someone was lent £2000 roughly on these terms they could end up paying back nearly £1950 in interest at a total cost of nearly £3950, not including other fees or charges.

To provide some context, a loan of £2000 from Sainsbury's Bank at a fixed interest rate of 18.6% APR, the total interest over the year would be £190.96, meaning the total repayable amount would be £2190.96. Even a comparable loan at the more expensive end of the scale from Halifax bank would cost you £2505.96 overall. It shows that even during rebranding exercises, the industry is expensive and destined to leave consumers with heavy debt.

Lord Parry's Win

Thank goodness, then, that industry critics won a crucial victory in December 2012. It was a long time coming; back in 2010 Stella Creasy MP, the foremost critic of payday lending in parliament, introduced the call for a cap on the total cost of credit (TCC) during a debate in the Commons on the Consumer Credit (Regulation and Advice) Bill. The TCC is different to capping interest rates because it takes into consideration all aspects of credit, such as administrative charges and other fees. In her submission to the BIS Consumer Credit and Personal Insolvency Review, Creasy indicated that late payment fees and auxiliary costs should be included in the maximum charge for credit.

So when the Financial Services Bill was passing through the House of Lords it was a good opportunity to raise the TCC again. Lord Parry Mitchell, a member of the shadow BIS team, former entrepreneur and now Ed Miliband's business ambassador and enterprise adviser, offered an amendment to the bill at a time when the coalition government were being extremely cautious (though some would say hostile) around accepting changes. Lord Parry was calling for the following powers for the Financial Conduct Authority (FCA - who will take over from the Office of Fair Trading regulating consumer credit on April 1 2014):

- To prohibit the charging of certain types of fees which it considers to be unacceptable;

- To prohibit the charging of costs above an amount which it specifies as unacceptable; and

- To prohibit rollover lending, where a debtor arranges separate credit arrangements in order to settle existing ones.

To much surprise the amendment was carried and as the bill passed through to being an act so the FCA had the powers to cap the cost of credit – a tremendous victory. Damon Gibbons of the Centre for Responsible Credit even called it an "historic moment". It was to be short lived.

The whole time campaigners and critics of the industry knew that since 2011 the Personal Finance Research Centre

(PFRC) at the University of Bristol had been writing a paper for the Department of Business, Industry and Skills about the operability of a cap on the cost of credit.[viii] It was also known that they are sceptical of such a move. The report was supposed to be published mid-way through 2012. I was due to interview the minister, at the time Ed Davey, about the findings of the report for the original publication of this book. I was told he would not speak to me until the findings were published. That would not be until March 2013, and Davey was replaced by Jo Swinson. On March 6, 2013 I receive a phone call at 07:00am. It was from Swinson's office to say that the report would finally be published that day. I was informed that there was no evidence to suggest a cap on the total cost of credit would benefit consumers who would find their supply of credit squeezed while demand was ever-growing. I was sent an embargoed copy of the report, as well as one by the OFT which had been published that same day, which I read cover to cover in under an hour. It was a strange thing that they were published side by side; while the OFT's found evidence of widespread irresponsible lending practices, culminating in the regulator writing to the 50 largest lenders (which accounts for 90 per cent of the UK market), BIS called only for small beer and cosmetic changes to be made.

Both reports were published at 10:00am, I rushed to Westminster to interview the minister for an allotted time of 15 minutes. The first question I asked was since the FCA have already been given the power to cap the cost of credit in the Financial Services Act 2013, which was due to come into effect (which it eventually did) on April 1, 2013, was this new report relevant? There was more than one reason why I had asked this question. I had been ringing the department in Bristol University where it was being written almost constantly asking where they were with the report. It wasn't said in so many words but the delay was to do with the government not agreeing with the report's conclusions. It came to my attention that BIS were preparing a report to be published simultaneously. In hindsight this becomes all the more interesting. Was it because of the amendment made to the act? Had the PFRC said anything complimentary about the need for a cap that BIS weren't happy with? The truth, I think, became apparent in Swinson's answer to me: "I think in looking at the wider remit of the FCA this report is relevant ... Nowhere else in the world is the total cost of credit capped, so we looked at the best practice across a range of countries".

When I showed Damon Gibbons the manuscript of the interview he laughed and said "well, that's not true". Indeed the Centre for Responsible Credit had recently published a report on lessons to be learnt from Japan where a TCC was introduced. It found that all things considered, putting a ceiling on the amount a lender can charge for a loan will make borrowing less expensive. In Japan there was no rise in illegal moneylending and in fact the total use of consumer credit overall dropped. The problem was that the minister took the PFRC as a blueprint of what the government should do. Indeed the official position of the government is that the FCA, while having that power, should not use it because it will be detrimental to consumers. However the PFRC/BIS report was not by any means a practical assessment of the strengths and weaknesses of a cap. Instead it was a very weak attitudinal assessment of a cap with information on interest rate caps as filler. Until an exhaustive piece of work has been carried out on this issue the government has no basis to make its assertion.

Neither, it should be said, does the FCA. To make matters more complicated the regulator published an Occasional Paper in April 2013[ix] which stated: "caps on APRs or restrictions on how often [consumers] can borrow might make their financial situation worse". It was made concrete now. Lord Parry's successful amendment was one step forward, but we immediately fell two steps back.

...And still the industry continued

The OFT had officially put the industry under an investigation, as mentioned in their report published March 6, 2013. This meant the industry had just 12 weeks from the time individual lenders received official letters with instructions to clean up its act. A small problem, however: the OFT took too long to send out the letters. Wonga posted an open letter[x] on its website saying they hadn't received their letter, just to rub it in – and I suppose in a strange sort of way who can blame them. Wonga get pilloried in the press, so when the regulator starts to muck up they are in there like a shot. It was around this time, in May 2013, that it was again brought forcefully home why there should be strong regulation over the industry – Wonga being no exception.

The company was all over the news when it had "raided" a 15 year old schoolboy's bank account[xi] after fraudsters had successfully applied for a loan with his details. In no way absolving the criminals who used Simon Oliver's account to obtain hundreds of pounds in loans, Wonga was called into question for the way in which it carries out its credit checks, via the magical algorithm. It is Wonga policy that they do not lend to under-18s – so how did this fall through their system?

Wonga are proud of their algorithm. So much so that they don't talk about it to journalists. One New York Times journalist I spoke to, who was busy writing a report on Errol Damelin, the Wonga chief executive, said she could not find any information on it at all and they weren't prepared to tell her anything. This is a common situation as far as external requests are concerned. Myself, I know it is comprises a collection of data points. For every applicant, Wonga says it can trace around 6-8,000 bits of information about them from credit reference agencies like Experian, paid-for information, and other social media information from such familiar places as Twitter and Facebook.

What remains to be seen is how Wonga, with such a huge resource, can allow such big loans to go through the system. This is Money carried out a noteworthy investigation[xii] months before Simon Oliver's case and found 41 people who collectively had over £30,000 taken from their accounts, met only with as the paper describes "a wall of silence from the lender".

Fraud against loan products rose quite significantly by 46 per cent from 2011 to 2012, and it is thought this represents and reflects the rise of payday lenders. One man I spoke to, Mark, was the victim of a fraudulent Wonga loan. According to him the lender had credit checked him specifically and then paid the money into another account, despite the fact he had never intended to ever use their service. He told me: "how can this happen if their system is as good as they frequently state?"

He continued: "I spent some time talking to Barclays about fraud, identity theft and the like and they definitely see this as a growing problem. I sensed some frustration in that some companies are treated different from an individual when applying to extract funds from an account. It would seem that they just don't have to go through the same checks".

Another person I spoke to, Andrew, told me that he was defrauded with Wonga loans on more than one occasion, being relieved of hundreds of pounds. When he took it up with Wonga he was offered a write-off settlement of a mere £100. This was after he had complained to the Financial Ombudsman Service. He suspects Wonga as having a policy of writing off all fraud under £5,000 – to avoid the media upshot. But thanks to continued pressure from defrauded people and concerned journalists Wonga fraud stayed in the press for a good while.

Wonga say that they take each and every fraud case seriously and that from time to time mistakes are going to be made, especially given the volume of loans they make. But perhaps the algorithm is just not the kind of success story they make out.

The magic bullet bill

On June 27, 2013 the entire payday lending industry was referred to the competition commission. The OFT had seen that not enough changes were being made and decided that the next level of scrutiny was necessary. This was good news. Focusing on competition would highlight an interesting side to payday lending that has been significantly neglected. High streets have already seen a "proliferation" of payday loans shops and this hasn't brought prices down for their customers. The simple reason for this is that lenders compete on speed. A shop that sells loans is not competing with a neighbouring shop on how much to sell you a loan for. Loans are consistently priced at around £25-35 per £100 borrowed over the period of 14 days. Instead payday lenders compete on the speed at which they can get money in your account. It is for this reason that many payday lenders find it difficult to reduce bad practices like failing to properly credit check a borrower. If the profit incentive is there to speed up the process and leave credit checking to one side then it will be hard for profit-making enterprises like payday lenders to break out of this bad habit.

The realisation of this seems to have already had an effect, too. At the time of writing 19 lenders of the 50 under investigation by the OFT have decided to leave the market. They include the likes of The Payday Loan Co Ltd (trading names include: Cashnet/ Paydayloan.co.uk/ Telecash/ The Payday Advance Company/ The Payday Loan Company); Speed-e-loans.com; Cash Advances Ltd (trading names include: Handycash/ Wagesstoday); and Hamilton Management Company Ltd (trading name: Anfield Cheque Cashing Services). Other lenders who were not even under investigation picked up and left, too. Keyring Ltd (trading name: Keycash); Paydaycredit Ltd (trading name: Submenow); and Geoffrey Michael Cavalier (trading names: Cash Express/ Post Box Express).

H&T Pawnbrokers also exited the payday loans market and will continue pawnbroking which is also regulated by the OFT. But they had another bit of bad news. They told the press that the cost of gold was hurting their business. Chief executive John Nichols said: "We took advantage of gold when it was going up and we did extremely well. That fuelled not only our expansion but a lot of others. With the declining gold price your margin is squeezed and you have to bring that price down and you have a double effect of less people wanting to sell their gold."

These companies, realising that a change was happening in regulatory scrutiny, found they were unable to play by the rules AND continue in the market. Coincidentally, only ten days earlier Paul Blomfield, MP for Sheffield Central, announced he would be leading a new move against rip-off money lenders, in the form of a Private Members Bill. The bill was set to be a necessary corrective to the *sat-on-hands* approach of the government. Only a few days before Blomfield's announcement Jo Swinson had set up a payday summit in which she invited representatives of the payday lending industry to talk through changes. It was sold as a chance for government to grill a controversial sector. Instead it was a love-in. Even in the presence of critics such as Martin Lewis and charities such as Citizens Advice, Swinson reiterated her government's commitment to avoiding a cap on credit. This is why the bill was vital.

Blomfield's bill included measures to set new rules around the affordability of loans, payday loan advertising, debt collection and payment, debt support, and penalties for companies who fail to comply with existing regulator guidance. The other strengths of the bill include setting advertising standards for the industry showing how much you could spend on a loan from a payday lender in pounds and pence, rather than at the annualised percentage rate (APR). Advertising would also have to show a "health warning" sign, to show that it is rarely the best form of credit to apply for in hard times. The bill calls for a freeze on all charges when a person with a payday loan misses a payment, the obligation for lenders to signpost free impartial advice on debt, and enforcement powers to be determined, such as compensation, if the details of this act (if it was to become an act) are breached.

Blomfield was suggesting what the government should have been committing to some months previous. The government knew this as well. Which is why the inevitable happened. On its second reading the government decided not to vote for it and the bill wasn't carried. Members of Parliament from Labour, Conservative, and the Liberal Democrat party came together to support the principles of the bill, and yet despite agreeing with the nuts of it the government decided to oppose it. Rumours abound that it did so to concentrate its efforts on a European referendum, something already agreed to in principle. In the fight between something with a real public interest and a backbench Tory obsession the backbench Tory obsession won. To parliament's shame.

Continued problems and promising developments

In 2013 alone there have been ups and downs that are worthy of a mention here. On the downside Chancellor George Osborne's budget speech made no effort to hide his attitudes to the poor. As George Eaton for the New Statesman put it: "Even after handing the highest earners an average tax cut of £100,000, the chancellor again had the chutzpah to claim that 'we're all in this together.'"[xiii] Osborne introduced a new seven day waiting period before somebody can receive benefit, making life even harder for those unlucky enough to not have a job. And as benefit payment is delayed further, and food banks are stretched to maximum capacity, the only option for some will be to turn to expensive short term credit on the high street. Chris Mould, executive chairman of the foodbank charity Trussell Trust, warned about the risk of delaying benefit payments saying: "Lots of people are referred to us because they already have problems with debts, many with short term loan organisations."

All the while credit unions had been given a boost. On top of DWP modernisation funds, mentioned elsewhere in this volume, come 2014 the financial institutions will have their interest rate cap raised slightly to make it easier for them to lend more money. The mandatory cap (ironically credit unions are the only financial institution in the UK where there are rules about how much interest they can receive when lending money) will now be raised from 26.8 per cent to 42.6 per cent, or from 2 per cent per month to 3 per cent per month. As financial journalist Paul Lewis said in a tweet when that announcement was made: "If an interest rate cap of 42.6% a year will let credit unions lend to more risky borrowers, why not impose same cap on all lenders?"[xiv]

A second boost came from a most unexpected place: God. That is to say God via the Archbishop of Canterbury. A paragraph in a relatively little known interview in Total Politics Magazine[xv] had the Archbishop Justin Welby announce that he had met with the chief executive of Wonga to tell him that the church wanted to help credit unions out-compete the company. It was going to do this by setting up its own, the Church of England credit union, and offering backroom space in churches for other credit unions to set up. The next moment it was big news. "Didn't Jesus go into the temple and throw out all the money changers"?, asked one commenter of a Telegraph article[xvi].

But of course credit unions offer lending with 'just' compensation; money made from a loan is not considered usury. One debate in biblical times and beyond was what constituted usury. Some felt it was moneylending full stop. Others, such as Thomas Aquinas, felt that for money made from a loan to be 'just', it could not profit anybody, as such, but compensate for operation costs.

The real problem for the Archbishop came less than 24 hours later. It was revealed in the Financial Times that the Church of England may have inadvertently funded Wonga through its own pension fund[xvii]. The reality however is not so black and white. The Church of England made commitments to a venture capital fund of funds in 2004 and 2007. This venture capital firm – Accel Partners – in 2009 was the leading firm who put up investment to start up Wonga along with The Wellcome Trust and others. I was told by the CoE press team that the total amount of exposure to Wonga is £75,000. I also spoke to an expert on these matters and they told me that "I'd read "exposure" to mean the amount CoE has invested in Accel divided by Accel's stake in Wonga".

In brief the CoE may have indirectly had its funds from the Church Commissioners Fund be exposed to the creation of Wonga in 2009. Since these commitments happened in 2004 and 2007 it would be impossible for the church to see in to the future and see what Accel would do. The point to be made here is whether ethical investment is ever completely guaranteed with private equity firms? Ask yourself this: do *you* know what your pension funds?

A victory – the work begins now

Other than the release of a Wonga film – a PR gimmick showing 12 testimonies from customers saying they were satisfied with the service – the last few months of 2013 (overall a very important year for the work against payday lenders) were relatively quiet for news on high cost credit. That was until Chancellor of the Exchequer did something quite unexpected.

From energy prices to cigarette packaging, Ed Miliband managed to dominate the political conversation – to the extent that right wing commentators in the Telegraph were saying

Conservative party u-turns were making their lack of conviction too obvious. In September 2013 Miliband was accused by David Cameron of 'living in a Marxist universe' when he suggested applying sensible regulations on the price of energy – a market that has demonstrably shown a severe lack of competition that has in turn impacted on prices for consumers which have been consistently too expensive, even before we benchmark them against the slow rise of wages.

However in November – quite out of the blue – George Osborne and the Treasury decided to say that it would place a cap on the cost of credit. To be sure, the regulator – the FCA – already had the power to cap the cost of credit, thanks to the aforementioned Lord Parry Mitchell. However Osborne announced that the cap will now be formally established through amendments made to the Banking Reform Bill.

The first thing the Labour leader did, during Prime Ministers Questions that week, was to accuse Cameron of suffering "an intellectual collapse". Not long after this the government put their tail between their legs and asked energy companies to lower their prices – which however you write it is an attempt to manage the markets at arms length – and so began the jeers that the Conservatives were simply stealing Labour's most popular policies.

As the Damascene conversion is to the better then we should resist jeers. Indeed as Miliband pointed out: "On May 22 2012 [the government] voted against capping payday lenders. On July 4 2011 [the government] voted against capping payday lenders. On February 3 2011 [the government] voted against capping payday lenders". They were wrong then, but now they have made amends.

Of course it is still interesting to see where this change of heart emerged from. It is a great philosophical shift, even from a sensible free market position, to say one minute that price regulation is akin to Marxism and then want to place a price ceiling on the amount financial services want to sell credit for.

One theory – a convincing one – is that the Government were worried they would lose a vote on it in the House of Lords. The Liberal Democrat peer and critic of the payday lending industry Lord Sharkey met with consumer ministers and tabled an amendment to the Banking Reform Bill which set a cap on the total cost of credit set at £300 and which allowed for no rollovers. Many crossbenchers, it seems, were unhappy that previous commitments to tackle the unfair practices of the payday loans industry were not made good, and it was certainly expected from within government circles that Sharkey could win his vote.

So, just in time Osborne called for the nuts of the amendment himself – something he knew was deeply popular in Labour camps and with voters. When the business department published their report on the cost of credit in March it said it had no further evidence itself on the effectiveness of a cap. The FCA, as I have mentioned, asked whether a cap would harm consumers. But even though evidence on this actually suggests price caps can benefit consumers, no further evidence prompted Osborne, only the political desire to appear on side of hardworking people – the politicians' buzzword of the day.

One country Osborne did mention as best practice when justifying the move is Australia. As I mention in greater detail in chapter 4 Australia is not the country to emulate. Even among consumer advocates the new protections in 2013 that stop lenders from charging exorbitant fees and interest charges were not enough to stop back door charges altogether. In fact some have suggested that plans to properly regulate the industry were watered down after a last minute decision to allow payday lenders to pass on fees for processing direct debits.

Even with an initial reform of payday loans prices across Australia, back in 2009, there were unintended consequences that the UK ought to learn from: namely that sham brokerage fees rose, cross-border lending became a real issue where a lender in one state lent to individuals in another that had stricter rules, and requirements to purchase 'financial literacy DVDs' were part of a loan contract. These were ways a lender could recoup what they saw as potential lost earnings from greater restrictions – and we need to look out for them in the UK.

***

Critics of the payday lending industry in the UK have been quick to celebrate the amendment to the Banking Reform Bill as a victory. And they are right to. This is a major achievement that could not have happened without the dedicated work of politicians, consumer advocates, and consumers themselves. But the work has not ended – in fact it has just begun. We now need to make sure that credit is capped at the right price. We need to see a cap on the cost of credit set at £12 per £100 borrowed – a figure that very carefully takes into consideration fairness for borrower and lender alike, and a break-even point for lending money to a more risky customer. We also need to address why it is that predatory lenders have profited so much off the back of the financially vulnerable, and hold companies to account of their own codes of conduct.

What happens now?

The Archbishop is absolutely right to take on Wonga and other payday lenders. But just because he wants to use competition doesn't mean he's against sensible regulation. Back in November 2012 Justin Welby himself, when he was the Bishop of Durham, called for a cap on the total cost of payday loans,[xviii] which is the definition of sensible legislation. Still, there is much to be frightful about with this industry, as I attempt to show throughout the rest of this book, and sadly this won't disappear now that the Treasury have agreed in principle to a price cap. Whatever our small victories, we must not rest while irresponsible credit lending and dangerous debt continues to rip through households and communities.

FOREWORD

Rowenna Davis, journalist, author of the book *"Tangled Up in Blue"*, and the Labour parliamentary candidate for Southampton Itchen.

BEING POOR is expensive.

Banks fall over themselves to lend to rich customers who promise large glittering deposits and low risks. They tempt them with sweet deals and low rates. The less well-off are treated very differently. Many at the bottom are denied credit from mainstream lenders, or forced to pay higher premiums. In the wake of the financial crisis, more of us are slipping into this category. We are compelled to find credit elsewhere. Payday loans are therefore on the rise.

In Peckham where I serve as a councillor, these companies are booming. In the throbbing concrete heart of South London, unstable employment and low wages force many of my constituents to payday lenders for basic goods – food, rent, nappies for children. I can reach five of these stores within a ten-minute walk of my flat. Shiny signs on their front doors promise interest rates as low as 25%; only the smallest print exposes APRs of over 1,000%.

Concerned about the impact of these stores, I decided to do some research of my own. In the spring of 2012 I posed as a customer to check how these companies were operating. The results were shocking. The checks were minimal, the full facts about the loan were often hidden and no situation seemed too bad to offer the money. For example, xxx was prepared to lend me £300 to bet on a horse race subject to a ten-minute credit check. This is part of the recorded transcript of the conversation:

RD: There's a horse that's going to win, so I can get it back to you this afternoon.

Lender: OK..

RD: So that's not a problem? If I come back in half an hour or something and bring that stuff, as long as I've been in my house a year it doesn't matter?

Lender: No.

RD: Brilliant! Thank you.

In another case I walked into xxx posing as a young woman who was struggling to pay the family rent after my mum got very ill and was forced to give up work.

The store was prepared to lend me almost £200, even though I said I had only been in work three weeks and the situation was going to get worse with a fixed rent contract. They recommended visiting other stores to make up the rest. When I added that I might be about to lose my job, the lender didn't flinch:

RD: Do you have to prove anything about future job prospects or anything like that? Because my work is just giving me so much grief.

Lender: You can give your work number but no one is going to call them or anything....

RD: I'm so worried because we're paying the rent together and we're in it for a year and if we can't pay it we're out basically. There's nothing we can do.

Lender: Go there (points to pay day loan shop next door) and
see how much they can give you and then calculate it with
this amount and it can make up the total. If you do it there
and do it here you'll be fine. You understand? The two will
make up the £400. Let me know. Come back..

Carl Packman's book is fantastic because it lifts the lid on
this industry and exposes the growing power that it wields.
Documenting the rise of the industry with detailed evidence,
Packman shows that, although there have always been loan
sharks, there has never anything as large and powerful as
the current set of payday loan companies operating virtually
unchecked in the mainstream of the UK.

But this book goes further than simply analysing the
problems: it also offers an honest discussion about practical
solutions. Packman raises difficult questions: for example,
whether credit unions should be permitted to raise their interest rate limits to justify costs to poorer lenders. Politicians
– most of whom tend to be in a stable economic position with
little experience of these companies – should take note.

Of course, irresponsible lenders will always exist as long
as people are poor. The Left should always fight the causes
of poverty that force people to accept devastating conditions
on credit. But as Packman exposes, it has become clear that
payday lenders are not just profiting from poverty; they are
adding to it. If we want to stop people getting into unsustainable debt, we have to give local people more power to limit these
stores, and to provide them with alternative, safe and cheap
means of accessing credit. The alternative is not just immoral.
It's unaffordable.

INTRODUCTION

1.75 MILLION adults in modern Britain do not have access to a transactional bank account. 7.7 million accounts are without credit facilities and a further 9 million people are without accounts that allow access to mainstream credit. Credit cards are dropping in circulation, by 1 million since 2011. PwC calls this the mid-life crisis of the credit card, which is currently seeing a contraction in use as the banking industry faces heavy competition from other financial products. This is all in spite of the rising costs of living, the job losses, the underemployment and the lack of a real wage increase for many workers.

What this reality has not been matched with is access to cheaper and better forms of lending. Credit union membership figures in the UK are around 2 per cent of the population, even with government funding and modernisation attempts. Compared to 24 per cent membership in Australia, 44 per cent in the United States and up to 75 per cent in Ireland, this does not bode well.

So how are people getting by?

We have seen a rise in the use of payday loans – an expensive financial product that has been widely criticized in recent times for the amount they charge borrowers. A report in the *Guardian* in 2011 showed that some payday lenders were charging what they called 60 times the "true cost of a loan"[1] – compared to a loan by My Home Finance, a not-for-profit organisation set up by the government and the National

1

Housing Federation in 2010, which charges a representative APR of 69.9%.

Online lenders such as Wonga, a well known lender of this variety, charge up to 4,214 per cent on a seven-day loan of £100, which means paying back around £112.78 to avoid late charges, or worse, suffer rollovers where additional loans need to be taken out to settle existing loan debts.

Payday loans often compare their prices to unauthorised bank loans, which can end up being comparably expensive, to give their product some justification. But compared with the average authorised overdraft charge, payday loans are expensive. The diagnosis here is not quite as simple as to simply say 'avoid those loans'. Many people are still priced out of enjoying mainstream credit, while living costs rise and wages are static. We should be demanding answers as to why so many people find it difficult to get to the end of the month without help from payday loans.

Sadly, such loans are the only alternative for some people.

In this book, I account for the phenomenal growth in UK payday lending (worth £100 million in 2004 to £1.7 billion in 2010), the political and economic context they operate in, and what must be done to tackle them. I focus on this in Chapter 3, with an eye to the personal debt landscape in Chapter 2. But it would be self-defeating to ban them outright. This is not desirable at all. *Illegal* loansharks are notorious for a reason, as addressed in Chapter 4.

Chapter 1 and part of Chapter 2 deal specifically with the history of credit, debt and some of the early historical arguments that preceded our present-day discussions about fair and responsible lending, and how we perceive the industry that lends consumers money today. The reason I have felt it necessary to deal with this history is because many current policy discussions are *simply not new*. I don't think this is fully appreciated, and we should feel enthused by the weight of historical and literary arguments against the exploitative and extortionate lending of today.

If it is the UK's modern payday lending industry you are primarily interested in, start at Chapter 3.

Chapter 6 deals with the alternatives to current payday lending, including credit unions, better and fairer banking, peer to peer lending and alternative economic systems. Chapter 7 offers conclusions and policy recommendations.

To paraphrase Robert Putnam, this volume offers no simple cures for our contemporary ills. But my principal motivation to write this book has been to shine a well-needed light on an industry that is growing at a rapid pace, and increasing, not alleviating, the anxieties and debt burdens of an ever-growing number of individuals.

Research by R3 has shown that 60 per cent of people who took out a payday loan have regretted the decision afterwards[2]. Indeed as I will show in the book, payday loans can very often be detrimental to an individual, and the companies themselves know it. I have aimed to clearly state the case why the industry needs better, stronger regulation and why I believe such financial products must be avoided.

Another motivation has been to bust many of the myths that exist. For example some well-meaning people have hastily assumed credit unions can fill in where payday lenders are operating. But unfortunately this is far too simple. From conversations I have had with credit union trade associations and other credit union professionals, the ability for them to lend to the same people as payday lenders will not be easy, and will take a drastic reconfiguration of their model. That is not to say, however, that this cannot be achieved, as I will go on to make clear in chapter 5.

Campaigning today, in particular from Stella Creasy MP and her fantastic signposting work on the issue, is not about banning payday lenders, but building up alternatives and raising consciousness. If I have done that, then I will be satisfied and hope to carry on the fight with the very many others who working to halt predatory lending.

Carl Packman
August 2012

CHAPTER 1

IN THE BEGINNING:
MONEY LENDING THROUGH
THE AGES

I HAVE SEEN fit to start the book by taking a look at the history, to illustrate how the image of moneylending has been shaped giving us a better sense of how payday lending is perceived today. The context here is very important. There is good reason why Paul Routledge for the *Daily Mirror* once said of payday lenders: "These Shylocks are the equivalent of Victorian pawnbrokers on street corners in the poorer areas of cities."[3] And I want to show that here.

However I would like to point out that if your interest is solely to do with payday lending and the UK context, I would encourage you to fast forward straight to chapter 3 where the specific discussion on the industry can be found.

***

Credit has always been a very confusing thing.

Not confusing in understanding how it works, but confusing in its impact on society. The image that credit evokes through history has only amplified this confusion. While the image of credit in the ancient world, as told by philosophers, might evoke "bans and shame", as Rosa-Maria Gelpi and François

Julien-Labruyère write in 'The History of Consumer Credit Doctrines and Practices',[4] credit was also the only means by which many could acquire goods and make purchases in the marketplace. Within religious communities (though one may think about the sin of usury), it was with Saint Thomas Aquinas that the Christian compromise on interest came about, as well as the concept of 'just' compensation that could be raised by a creditor.

For nearly every story about credit in the past, there is a counter-narrative. To say that there was a single way in which credit was viewed in the ancient world and through to the Middle Ages is as erroneous as suggesting that credit is a recent development.

While the image of credit, lending, personal debt and profits raised on payments has a negative image, it is very interesting how such matters were generally thought of in the past. Popular histories and literary figures have done the most to raise our consciousnesses to how such things were previously considered and shape our opinions as to how far we have come.

It's easy to think of how negatively perceived the money-lenders were, how villainous Shylock was in Shakespeare's The Merchant of Venice, and how noble a demand it was to give to one's brother without the expectation of profiting personally. But it was never so black and white. The debates and discussions on matters of finance were very rich indeed, and there is much to learn from them. Cliché as it is, history *does* tend to repeat itself. It is for this reason that I have chosen to contextualise this book with financial history. This adds resonance to more contemporary debates we have around personal debt, and, alas, we often find that familiar truism repeats itself – first as tragedy, then as farce.

Many current debates have been had before. How much a person should reasonably be able to profit from lending, as well as the ethics of the business, are as old as financial transactions themselves. Issues concerning what measures to take when payments are deferred are no more unfamiliar to history than war and conflict. The following section develops ideas of historical legacy, public and intellectual attitudes, and what challenges arose on the subject in the past, for consumer credit. It shows that those very same complaints about injustice concerning debtors, and the efforts that lawmakers went to in order that this be rectified, or indeed maintained, have all happened before, and that rather than deterring us from the struggle for fairness, it should remind us of the historical legitimacy of our demands.

What follows is not exhaustive, and is certainly not my own original research, but is intended to provide an overview and a commentary on those important events that have shaped our understanding of the history of credit.

Ancient usury – the shape of things to come

You expect to find that life was harder in the past. Certainly on the subject of debt in the ancient world, there is a lot of truth in this, but on the other hand, there are also positive elements. For example, in Ancient Babylon, aside from the horrors of child slavery and concentrated riches, peasants were not ordered to pay back capital or interest on debt in the event of a long spell of flooding or drought. There were many other upsides, too, such as the view that land and goods must not be forfeited to private creditors, on the grounds that this would have ultimately weakened the kingdom militarily (for example, under the Code of Hammurabi – a Babylonian law code, dating back to around 1772 BC).

Loans in Babylon, for example, would be provided interest-free between family members, business partners and other colleagues, and it was typical for aristocrats to lend to each other interest-free through *eranos* clubs. Generally speaking, among Mesopotamian rulers, it was thought that the dynamics of interest-bearing debt were not self-stabilising, according to Michael Hudson, a research professor at the University of Missouri. Therefore in order to apply their own very simple stabilising mechanisms, rulers intervened by annulling unpayable debts. Just like that. As Hudson writes in 'The New Economic Archaeology of Debt',[5] modern wisdom sees fit to punish debtors by obliging them to forfeit land and goods to the rich, in some cod-Darwinian shift of property from the lesser off to the wealthy. This, according to the Babylonian leaders, did not make good economic sense.

Of course, this did not mean it was a society free of victims of debt. In fact, if a debtor were to be seized for debt, the punishments were severe. The debtor had the option of nominating as 'mancipium', or hostage to work off the debt, his wife, child, or slave (peonage). The rules here were pretty simple. If, while under the care (care being used in the loosest sense of the word) of the creditor, the mancipium died, then the latter could remain free and no claim could be made against him. However, if the creditor was the one who caused the death, say through his own neglect or careless hand, it would then be incumbent upon him to either give up his own child or purchase a slave for the debtor.

Although such treatment of debtors and their families appears abominable to the modern reader, the attitude by the rulers at the time regarding how unproductive debt was to wider society indicates an advanced understanding of the subject. Curiously, the Mesopotamians did not ban usury – they only intervened at the point at which debt became uncontrollable. In Mesopotamia circa 2400BC, usury was common practice. Michael Hudson, again in his essay 'The New Economic Archaeology of Debt', notes that the Mesopotamians also appeared to anticipate the classical distinction between productive and unproductive lending. The difference here is that loans where the creditor is able to provide the borrower with enough so that he can pay back with interest, like 'silver-loans' to merchants would do, were productive. Debts of the other major monetary commodity – barley – which were represented in consumer loans were not considered so profitable, and under the Babylonians, the Sumerians and in subsequent economies, were summarily annulled. Through canon law, churchmen of the Middle Ages identified the differences between lending to the poor and lending to the rich, but the Bronze Age Mesopotamian rulers differentiated between productive and unproductive lending.

Opposition towards usury appears noble enough – why should anybody be making personal gains over and above the service they have given? And writing off debts so as to maintain societal harmony and financial stasis seems admirable. But those two things never lived a life side by side with the Mesopotamians. Only "faced with the potential for complete social breakdown [did] Sumerian and Babylonian kings periodically announce general amnesties"[6], says David Graeber, anarchist anthropologist and reader in Social Anthropology at Goldsmiths, University of London. The implication is that, rather than these rulers applying a financial regulatory system that saw off crises for the lesser off, amnesties were infrequent and exercised primarily to avoid further work to build up from complete social breakdown, not to maintain balance. But whether for good reasons, or good through by-product, after a certain time all land was returned to its original owners, and debt peons were returned to their families. No coincidence, then – and certainly not one lost on Graeber – that the Sumerian word *amargi* is the first recorded use of 'freedom' in any language, literally meaning 'return to mother', as were the freed debt peons.

Part of the appeal of David Graeber's work is the counter-narrative he gives for the creation of money and credit, particularly in his book 'Debt: The First 5000 Years'.[7] Graeber argues there is nothing new or novel about virtual money – this was the *original* form of money. The only thing that stands out as unique with today's virtual credit world is that there is a reluctance to apply the sort of debt forgiveness that had been present in places like Mesopotamia. Today there is usury without amnesty.

But the most interesting conversations about usury, what it is and whether it is right or wrong, had yet to be had.

Usury and just compensation – the religious conversations on finance ethics

In 'Politics', Book I, Part 10, Aristotle opined of usury: "Wherefore of any modes of getting wealth this is the most unnatural".

Undoubtedly based on how absurd making personal fortune through money deals would have seemed at the time, the philosopher could not find the words to explain why it was that he had such visceral doubts about usury. But where Aristotle had the passion, people of a religious persuasion were able to offer an ethical and systematic description of why usury was sin. But this is only half the story.

When one thinks about the kind of commands contained in religious scripture, say the Bible, on matters of conducting oneself financially and ethically, then one perhaps is reminded of Luke 6:35, which holds: "But love ye your enemies, and do good, and lend, hoping for nothing again; and your reward shall be great, and ye shall be the children of the Highest: for he is kind unto the unthankful and to the evil." To this end, doing good where no personal gain is necessarily extended will eventually be rewarded with something far greater than mere wealth – namely, to be numbered as a child of God in Heaven after passing through life.

This was not the end of the story in the church's debate on usury. Saint Thomas Aquinas was the first to propose a compromise in the church, with opponents of usury on one side and advocates of interest on the other. Later this journey would come to be linked to Christianity after the reformation period – and had far-reaching conclusions. As author John Paul Davis told me: "The evolution of banking depended heavily on the change in regulation that occurred post-Reformation regarding usury".

According to Lendol G. Calder, at the Department of History in Augustana College, Rock Island, throughout the 16th century and beyond, legions of short-sighted theologians and philosophers tried to strangle credit with religious dogma, with the result that credit was: "More or less forbidden but more or less practiced because more or less necessary"[8].

While tied to good ethical ground, society and even religious communities started to see an end in the economic credibility of banning interest on all loans. Something had to give, and for it to be acceptable, it had to be clothed in Christian threads.

Aquinas acknowledged that there could be limited legitimate compensation for loss to capital (damnum emergens). According to Constant J. Mews and Ibrahim Abraham in their essay 'Usury and Just Compensation: Religious and Financial Ethics in Historical Perspective',[9] discussions on usury had developed by Franciscan and Dominican friars as the growing awareness of regulation was needed after the 'credit boom' of the 12th century. In medieval Europe, says Michael Hudson, the Church lifted its ban on usury initially to permit the revival of lending for foreign trade, in the form of the *agio* charged for converting payments from one currency to another. Even in the Christian community, disallowing people from profiting from lending was not clear-cut – there were times when it was perfectly acceptable to do it, and this increased as the economic conditions changed to suit. Stephen James, writing for *News Review* on charging high rates of interest to the less wealthy in California, pointed out clearly that: "Over time – to accommodate the expansion of capitalism, commercialization, international trade and other economic factors – a pro-usury counter-movement began to take hold."[10]

It was after this point, for the Christian world and for its financial ethics, that the meaning of usury shifted, "from one referring to any loan with an interest charge to one referring to a loan with an exorbitant interest rate."[11]

A similar story can be found in the Hindu religion. According to Stephen James, the oldest references to usury are in the Vedic texts, religious manuscripts dating from 1,500 BC. Here usury is defined as any loan that obliges the one who is lent to service an interest payment. However, by the second century AD reasonable fees for loans were permitted and the Hindu definition of usury modified to put more focus on socially acceptable sums for interest payments.

The way in which loans were allowed and what further costs could be permitted did shift, but not back to how the ancient world did it, where usury was open. Instead, it prepared for what was considered to be the type of society to come – one that needed credit, as well as needing mutual benefit for creditor and debtor. Within Christian circles, the principles of finance needed to be systematic as much as they required emphasis derived from religious teaching. Changing to meet the new financial landscape, a Christian could still be a Christian and tolerate interest payments, providing a number of other criteria were met. Deuteronomy 24:6 states that:

"No man shall take the nether or the upper millstone for a pledge: for he taketh a man's life to pledge."

In other words, no man should take away from another man the means he has to support himself in at least the most basic way. What developed from here was the importance of how lending was conducted. Clearly, in order to maintain values, while avowedly distancing itself from its previous flat opposition to usury, the Christian community had to promote and pursue good lending over predatory lending. It is within this context that we situate the societal and cultural backlash against the loan shark.

14th century Italy – the struggle between legitimate and black market lending

800-600 BC saw the creation of coinage (as well as all the major religions), while the Middle Ages, 600-1500 BC, saw a return to virtual credit. Game-changing discussions had been had by this time, and the Christian church seemed to consent to a reasonable level of just compensation attached to loans, albeit with a guilty consensus. The etymological root for the word credit (*credo*) is 'I believe' – but belief was not enough, as the world of finance became more sophisticated. In Venice, there was great exposure to the Orient, where trade and importing was a booming industry. It also provided a location for what was to be the next chapter in the moneylending experiment: the rise of banks. This experiment was one based on shame and reluctance, to say the least. It gave rise to many heroes and villains in the lending industry. Rosa-Maria Gelpi and François Julien-Labruyère noted that even "Giotto created the whole cycle of frescos of the famous Scrovegni Chapel in Padua to prevent his sponsor from erring towards the infernal path of usury." Usury remained a dirty word to the Christian church, but it was also wise to what lay in wait if there had not been a socially acceptable – and Christian – mode of lending.

In 14th century Venice, with the rise of banks came great power and influence for the Medici family. Under the Medicis, credit is said to have come of age and "money became glorious", according to historian Niall Ferguson. The family was granted its noble status in Italy not because they were charging interest, for which there was the real risk of committing sin, but by levelling commission. Interest payments were thus discreetly concealed and the world of moneylending – which stuck in the throats of Christians – turned into the mainstream art of banking. Merchant bankers through the ages had been accused of taking advantage of the Christian canon law by raising the notion of legitimate loss to capital and compensation.

According to Constant J. Mews and Ibrahim Abraham, if they had been guilty of taking money from the poor through usury, the way they could salve their conscience was through philanthropy. What was unique about the Medici family and the rise in banking to which they were linked, was that they did not try to overcompensate by doing seemingly philanthropic acts, but simply by rebranding and concealing usury, and making folk devils of those lending money at sky-high rates. And, of course, there was a religious narrative here;– witness the most notorious moneylender in fictional history – Shylock.[12]

As Rosa-Maria Gelpi and François Julien-Labruyère have noted, usurers represented in literature from Shakespeare to Dante remain the same: "pale, spiteful and greedy". In Dante's Inferno, usurers were consigned to the seventh circle of hell. Interestingly, what has frequently been noted of Shylock is that he is driven to usury not through an unhealthy pursuit of profit, but by vengeance. Wanting his pound of flesh, is interesting, since flesh and money were considered comparable at the time Shakespeare was writing, but also gives the impression that Shylock is not expecting to receive what he would consider his just desserts, but more than that – a stake in another individual that would satisfy his desire to avenge.

Shylock's trade did lend itself to vengeance. In her essay 'Shylock and the Slaves: Owing and Owning in The Merchant of Venice',[13] Amanda Bailey notes that forfeiture in the 17th century was a very serious thing, and when a person could not pay back a free (without interest) debt they would either give up their liberty or life. Given how extreme this punishment seems, it is understandably odd to learn that within Shakespeare's play was a lesson in the difference between debt – or the ideal of ethical ownership – and usury. Bailey recounts that money, being a non-fungible form of property, like land or chattels, meant that loans on bond could not be negotiated via substitution or exchange. For her, conceptually debt here parts ways with usury, precisely because usury involves transfer of ownership, rather than the leasing of something to somebody else.

A crucial aspect of the play is how the actions of Shylock highlight the crucial difference between taking out a loan with interest – what John Locke later identified as 'usufruct', meaning the ideal of ethical ownership, seen as the righteous response to the more morally dubious aspects of ownership – and signing up to a debt bond where ownership is acquired by degrees. Bailey notices that there is no question of Shylock's legitimate claim to own Antonio's person – one's own person, one's pound of flesh was, as previously mentioned, comparable, and written in Shylock's conditions for lending (consider, for example the scene in which Shylock repeats the terms of a loan to Bassanio, before Bassanio is asked whether Antonio is 'good' in the sense of the word that would imply safe to lend to, i.e. are they good for it?). Debt bondage, which this play illustrated, necessitated a new-found urgency in the state's role in preserving an inalienable right to life, even if the market was allowed to perpetuate alienable right to property of person. Even though a creditor had unresting interest in a debtor's person, the state acted by maintaining that no debtor could forfeit his right to life. This, of course, did not mitigate for debtors spending out their days in prison, but a state that ensures life itself is not a disposable object for debt is a more civilised one.

The law in 'The Merchant of Venice' recognises Shylock's right to a pound of flesh, but also recognises that Antonio's blood ought to be spared. In the eyes of the court, it also bears out, in having his pound of flesh, Shylock would actually be murdering a Christian – Shylock only escapes by submitting to baptism.

Another example, whether man or myth, who certainly adds to the history and evolution of banking, and definitely adds so much to the historical narrative of Britain, is Robin Hood, a figure best known for his commitment to taking from the rich and greedy to give to the poor and needy. In 2010 a *Telegraph* review article entitled 'New book claims Robin Hood stole from the rich and lent to the poor.'[14] The review was for a book called 'Robin Hood: The Unknown Templar', the author of which, John Paul Davis, told me that while he "does not make any claim that the historical outlaw, should he have definitely existed, was a loan shark - my views being less flamboyant - [...] according to the ballad A Gest of Robyn Hode, Robin Hood, a yeoman, waylays a knight, suggesting he can offer him a loan after the knight has admitted to losing his wealth while being in the debt of the abbot of St Mary's in York.".

The story goes that Robin Hood, a man of common status, dines with the knight before insisting he pay his fair share for the meal on the grounds that a yeoman should never pay the bill of a man of higher status. Robin, on finding out about the knight's lost wealth, offers not to pay but to lend him the money himself with security. The knight, having no possessions to offer as security, pleads that only the Virgin Mary can act as security, which Robin duly agrees to. A year later and Robin Hood and his merry men want their money back, but the knight has fled. Robin then steals from the abbot, justifying this on the grounds that the abbot is greedy. When eventually the knight returns to pay back the loan, Robin Hood refuses to accept it, noting that the Virgin Mary has been true to her word. (As Robin Hood was a Templar he swore a vow of poverty, but in spite of this he still charged a fee for his loans, some as high as 10%).

Using the aforementioned ballad to back up his controversial claims, Davis points out that loans were the sole preserve of the Templars and the Jewish moneylenders in the Middle Ages, and Robin Hood himself had a decent amount of money that he was willing to lend out. He would largely lend to the needy, but he didn't just give it away as, but lent at reasonable rates from funds mostly stolen from those Robin would have considered the 'unworthy'.

What must be taken into account is that the Templars, though making money from lending stolen money to the poor, were bound to a certain Christian morality which prohibited harm to other Christians – the implication being that extortion was probably not in practice. Davis notes that, in stealing from the abbot, Robin Hood himself was not always observant of this.

Throughout the ages, the right to enjoy credit was fought for as a means to participate in society and enjoy some of the luxuries, previously the preserve of the rich. Credit became a class issue. The working classes were running against the tide in their pursuit of credit, not least because of the perception that its use implied financial imprudence or poor morality. Even before returning to exploitation through moneylending, we see that part of the fight was for the poor to be recognised as a dignified element to the growing economy in the West. We also learn that the noble efforts of that fight have since been used to excuse extortion now banks are going through another phase of risk aversion.

Edwardian and Victorian era debtors – the forgotten British class war

Fast forward a few hundred years, and with the rise in consumer credit, the image of Shylocks exploiting people was sidelined in favour of the view that, in general, people taking out loans and getting into debt was a product either of an individual's succumbing to vice, or worse, the inability to handle themselves financially, which carried an enormous stigma, particularly in the Edwardian and Victorian eras.

Frank Trentmann in his paper 'Beyond Consumerism'[15] describes an alternative vision of consumption, which subsequently went on to shape the development of capitalist society, driven by "ideals of the citizen-consumer". Erika Rappaport's significant study of shopping in London's West End in the late 19th and early 20th century shows that, rather than the new culture of consumption being necessarily predicated on commercial exploitation or oppression, shopping was an activity solely for harmless pleasure. But more than that, as Rappaport noted, shopping became an emancipatory activity through which middle-class women defined a new sense of bourgeois feminine identity, carved out new public spaces, and became energised as political actors.

It was, however, an exclusive world, a world which needed the poor to facilitate it – to work the shops, to produce the materials – but which they were unable to enter into. Credit, already in circulation, could be used by the middle classes without fear of stigma to allow for expenditure on consumables, but access to credit for the working class was seldom so accepted and mainstream. Many, of course, were stopped from taking it out, instead relying on Provident (who provide home credit), a small cash or voucher loan company, or pawnbrokers, which cost more and led to more financial difficulty.

Pawnbroking in the Edwardian and Victorian era was a very female-oriented affair. Husbands would be busy at work, while women, left at home to get on with their 'duties', would often be in charge of pawning off items for that extra bit of income. The routine was to pawn the families' best clothes on Monday, use the money during the week and then buy the clothes back for Saturday night or Sunday's religious festivals.

Another source of credit could be acquired through informal savings clubs in working men's clubs. Ruth Cherrington, a historian who has specialised in working men's clubs, spoke to me about unofficial savings clubs that have existed since the 19th century:

"Clubs collected the membership subscriptions, or subs, once a year, usually in January or February. They also ran various savings clubs such as for Christmas, and men and women put aside bits of money through these clubs. The short-term hedonism of working class life meant that saving for the future was not a part of the culture but clubs since the 19th century tried to encourage savings in these small but important ways." Dr Cherrington also points out that "Most working class people back in the 50s, 60s and probably into the 80s didn't have bank accounts. If they needed money, they would have to rely on loans from contacts or known money lenders, often in clubs".

But the accusation this was all down to poor budgeting by vulnerable families doesn't tally with the evidence. Maud Pember Reeves wrote about the "ordinary working class" in her account Round About a Pound a Week which surveyed the years 1909-1913. She deliberately wrote not about the neediest, but the lives of manual labourers and families working at ordinary levels of pay. The pound they lived off of would be the equivalent to £370 in today's money, which is around £19,250 per annum. Far from being spent on beer, tobacco and gambling she witnessed meticulous budgeting by the women trying to keep their children healthy and provide their husbands with decent meals. Part of Pember Reeves' study found families putting money into local funeral insurance schemes, highlighting the "social stigma of a pauper's funeral". Her study also captured the importance of the informal economy – the loans of money and food between neighbours and families when some fell on hard times.

This is the really important point to make, and very much worth remembering for today: those on low incomes are very often better budgeters than many would have us believe. When I asked about the arguments that tended to be levelled at people in 1700-1800s who found themselves with high levels of debt, Margot Finn, a historian at the university of Warwick and author of the seminal work 'The Character of Credit: Personal Debt in English Culture, 1740 – 1914',[16] told me:

"On the one hand, forgiving debt could be viewed as virtuous (the translation of the Lord's Prayer used in the 18th century read 'Forgive us our debts...') but what we must remember is the upper classes bought virtually everything on credit, being charged every 6-12 months, so that being in debt could be a sign of being upper class. On the other hand, especially in business, not meeting one's obligations, not being credit-worthy, was a stain."

Being on the wrong side of considered opinion of the day, dominated by a quick-to-judge middle class morality, is one thing; but being met with this in court is quite another. Decisions about small debts – which attracted the poorest class of debtors – remained unjustifiably strict, if not openly vindictive. This had much to with Victorian morality and was subject to questions of a debtors' personal morality, with the touchy accusation of gambling, as well as imprudence, being levelled by everyone from the press to the courts.

In his wonderful study of credit, debtors and Victorian England,[17] Paul Johnson recalls the 1853 case of Blackstone vs. Turner, which involved Thomas Turner, an agricultural labourer and part-time town crier of Wallingford, Berkshire, and the granddaughter of the eminent English jurist, Sir William Blackstone, referred only to as Miss Blackstone. Turner was alleged to have attacked Miss Blackstone, while also relieving her of £30, after a legal dispute between her and Turner's brother, William, over the renting of allotment gardens. It was said in court that he did also make use of "some very opprobrious expressions unfit for any women to hear".

The case here is interesting because it reveals many of the biases of the procedure in lowly civil courts. Turner denied the incident took place, but admitted to having used bad language, while Judge J B Parry QC had already made up his mind, saying: "If every person in that court had been called and said they did not see the defendant strike the plaintiff, it could not have countervailed the evidence of unimpeached witnesses."

The problem was that, even in spite of the supposedly unimpeached witnesses, the evidence was stacked against the accusation. An anonymous Wallingford justice of the peace noted in a letter to the *County Courts Chronicle* that there had been "a great discrepancy of the evidence produced, and several credible witnesses swore positively that no assault had been committed". It was revealed in Dod's 1853 *Electoral Facts* that the Blackstone family had a considerable amount of influence in their day, not least Miss Blackstone's brother, William Seymour Blackstone, who was "the Deputy Lieutenant for Berkshire [and] had been the Conservative MP for Wallingford for the twenty years from 1832". But even before this final revelation, we can see that here the verdict is a clear favouring of, in the words of Paul Johnson, "the word of a person of standing above that of a labourer".

Unsurprisingly, Judge Parry awarded damages at a maximum sum of £50, plus costs, and demanded it be paid to Miss Blackstone immediately. Turner couldn't pay, had all his possessions seized, and sale of them turned around just £3 and 3s. Turner was ordered to pay off his debt at 6s per month, which would have dominated his incomings. Indeed, he ended up defaulting on the first payment, and due to additional charges, after appearing before Judge Parry again later in the year, was owing £63 12s 9. The unjust case went all the way to Lord Palmerstone, who called the case one of great hardship and cruelty, but this fell on deaf ears. The *County Courts Chronicle* excused the ordeal on the grounds that the judge was acting within the law, despite the official assessment that Turner had the means to pay 6s back per month from earnings of 14s 8d a week, while maintaining his wife and five dependent children aged between 18 months and 15 years.

Turner was sentenced to virtual life imprisonment for his failure to pay back his debt and as a leading article in *The Times* concluded: "Under an appearance of justice to all classes, it presses hardly on some."

Between 1847 and 1914, over 98 per cent of cases were for sums of less than £20, with an average amount owing of around £3. Of course, at the time, perpetrators of such crimes had a specially designated prison, designed just right to punish them: these were debtors' prisons.

As we are reminded in Johnson's work: "Arrest on final process had been abolished for debts of less than £20 in 1844, but in 1845 this liberalising measure was reversed by a new act which designated as fraudulent any debt contracted by an individual lacking any reasonable prospect of being able to pay; a condition which applied to most working-class debtors most of the time."

One notable person to have narrowly missed the brief period in which small debtors avoided prison was the father of one of our most treasured writers in history. Charles Dickens was 12 years old, putting labels onto bottles for a living, when his father was sent to debtors' prison. Unknown to his contempories, two of Dickens' most famous characters were actually based upon his father: David Copperfield and Mr Dorritt, an inhabitant of a debtors' prison in 'Little Dorritt'.

At the time many of the debtors' prisons were rather modern buildings – indeed the prison Dickens' father was sent to was built in 1811. The prisoners were treated rather fairly, and even alcohol was on sale! A pint of wine or two pints of beer could be consumed daily, but spirits were officially banned, although black market whiskey could be had. One of the prison guards in 'Little Dorritt' says: "Strikes me that imprisonment for debtors is a holiday."

The staff in the prisons often had no other role than to forcibly stop people from escaping, although many did. A most notable example of this had been Lord (Thomas) Cochrane, a radical politician in his day and the 10th Earl of Dundonald, who after escaping handed himself back in on 6 March 1815, later paid his debts, then became a naval officer in Chile. It was in 1813 that the insolvency act made headway into better dealing with debtors' prisons – remembering that when a person went to prison, nobody benefitted – neither the prisoner nor the person to whom a debt was owed. Though it took until 1860 to see most of the prisons knocked down or used for other purposes, by 1869 they were all gone. Dickens visited one of the more notorious ones, Marshalsea (which had closed in 1843), after finishing 'Little Dorritt'. Responding to the sight of it he is reported as saying it was "very little altered".

The courts were also out for the small debtors who struggled to live by their own means alone, and who had only to look around them at the newly built sites hosting the advent of consumer capitalism and a new, exclusively middle-class culture of consumption, to see reflected the excess and greed of which they themselves were being accused. The use of Provident loans, though the only alternative, was self-defeating as it did not ever afford the kinds of consumable luxuries that were becoming a feature of many better-off households.

A 1908 *Daily Mail* report patronisingly suggested that "people who mostly use this system [Provident loans] are naturally the working man". The sea-change becomes obvious. Back when Christianity had an influence on financial matters the lender bore the burden of moral turpitude. Now Christian values, by way of the perceived Victorian and Edwardian value system, were being used as a way to question the morality of the debtor, to the extent where it was seen as fit and proper to deny them a free life. Today, nobody goes to prison for owing £20, or even the modern-day equivalent, but the same stigma is attached. To be sure, there are still enough people today who would consider a person entering into debt as financial imprudence alone, without gathering the proper context, or appreciating that the lender has to share in the blame too, as was generally considered in the period that produced Shylock.

CHAPTER 2
CONSUMERISM, THE RISE OF THE
LEISURE CLASS AND THE AGE OF
BAD DEBT

THERE HAS been considerable debate as to when precisely consumer consciousness first emerged and, judging by wage spending patterns, whether or not the consumer revolution had taken place *before* the industrial revolution. One thing we can say for sure is that this revolution was geared primarily toward the middle classes of the day, while the working class waged an often fruitless battle to access the luxuries afforded to those on relatively higher incomes.

The term consumerism has not stayed with a single meaning over the years – in 1915, in its first recorded usage in the Oxford English Dictionary, it's referred to as 'advocacy of the rights and interests of consumers', but has modified over time to mean something rather more preoccupied with the acquisition of goods and services. To be sure, there have always been consumers and consumption, but something in consumerism seemed to come of age, especially from the 1960s onwards. Movements that have developed and evolved in the West actively campaigning against consumerism have not been protesting against consumption, but the changing nature of consumer society, based on supply and demand. Such movements have usually targeted 'culture jamming' (a tactic used to subvert mainstream cultural institutions, including corporate advertising) and the way in which corporations have targeted advertising towards different consumers that aims to convince individuals that their life could change significantly for the better if they buy a particular product.

In the words of Adorno and Horkheimer, the consumer becomes a passive participant in the "culture industry" and trapped in a "circle of manipulation and retroactive need"[18].

When Karl Marx rallied against what he saw as commodity fetishism in the late 19th century, his sights were on the relations that took place between humans wholly or partially mediated through objects or things such as commodities or money. In psychoanalysis, fetish as a concept denotes something that is enjoyed for reasons above and beyond its natural or intended use or value. A foot, for example, is used to walk, but the foot-fetishist enjoys the foot for reasons entirely different to the foot's actual purpose and attaches to it other subjective meanings from which he gains sexual pleasure. As far as consumerism is concerned, materials and consumer goods that take on wholly artificial meanings, and are as far removed from their original intent or utility purpose, instead taking on absurd life-forms, accounting for commodity fetish.

Marx is more relevant today than he has ever been. Michael Billig in his paper on commodity, fetishism and repression,[19] notes that Marx's analysis of commodities implies a kind of collective amnesia that neglects to remember the productive origins of commodities – a reflection, Marx felt, of capitalism. Today, Billig argues, this is even more the case than it was when Marx was undertaking his examinations. Consumer-focused groups and campaigners, such as those responsible for fair trade campaigns or ethical consumerist markets, are trying all the time to ensure consumers are aware of where their consumer goods are coming from, in order to raise their consciousnesses about exploitation (sweatshops and unfairly traded goods from the third world being examples), but what consumer capitalism

is essentially aiming at is for the consumer to not only buy into
unrealistic lifestyles, but to forget the social relations that have
taken place in the creation of a product or good.

Consumption is never just consumption

As early as the turn of the 20th century, consumption is never
just consumption: there is generally some explanation that
underpins the way in which it is done. For Thorstein Veblen,
consumption, or to use his concept of 'conspicuous consumption', is carried out for its social value rather than its intrinsic
product benefits or personally inscribed meanings. Rather
than consuming for its necessity alone, there becomes an added
value attached. An obvious example is the designer bag which,
though something in which vital objects such as keys, purses,
pens can be placed and carried about with ease, takes on an
entirely different status, namely that the individual wearing it
is of a certain social class, can afford certain luxury goods and
knows, at the end of the day, how to waste money with style.

Critics of Veblen suggest that this is a rather old fashioned
way of looking at consumerism – indeed Veblen was writing
this in his 1899 book 'The Theory of the Leisure Class'.[20] For
the so-called postmodern consumer theorist, fragmentation,
pastiche and bricolage stamped out consistency and single-
mindedness which previously connected the status system
– "shunning conventional (upscale) status aspiration", as the
contemporary consumer theorist Juliet Schor puts it. This is
fairly easy to identify. Even aside from the fact that we identify
certain objects or goods as synonymous with a certain social
status which abstracts wholly from the original intent of the
good itself, the connotation that that particular good brings up
does not stay the same forever. For example, a leather jacket has
the useful quality of keeping one warm, but looked at through
the lens of a cultural critic, it can also denote a tough, James
Dean-esque figure whom other men are scared of and the girls

love. The postmodern consumer theorist would add to this reading that the modern-day leather jacket-wearing individual does not necessarily want to be seen as a James Dean-esque figure, but rather, is wearing the jacket ironically. The James Dean-esque interpretation must not be ignored, but it is only one aspect of the reading.

The same reading may be attached to clothes that have previously defined someone as one particular class. The top hat was once the sole preserve of the upper-class chap, making sure that he stood out from the lower-class majority, leagues beneath him in status. This does two things simultaneously: it fetishises the point of a hat (principally to keep one warm) and also defines social standing. Wearing a top hat today does not necessarily do that, because consistency (this object means this, another object means that) has been obscured by consumer fragmentation and irony.

What we often mean when we refer to consumerism today is over-consumption, or consumer capitalism, which comes with its own set of assumptions about the necessity of available consumer goods, whether we are, again in the words of Adorno and Horkheimer, duped into the circle of manipulation.

An interesting study that took place by Elliot, Eccles and Gournay[21] which illustrates just how removed the consumption of everyday life is to what we refer to when we talk about consumerism, concerned a group of individuals who self-identified as being addicted to the 'consumer experience'. The participants, who were noted to have 'unmanageable' credit card and other debts, were identified as having characteristics suggesting a struggle for power and control within relationships, often using over-spending as a means of revenge, particularly where partners were picking up the tab, so to speak.

The interviews (46 with women and four with men, which does raise problems in itself) found that purchases were made for motives not directly related to actual possession of goods themselves, even in a research sample of very mixed income ranges. One very well-off participant, Julie, 36, had been the youngest of four children and admitted she was her father's favourite. Her husband, a GP, paid off all her credit card bills, admitting that she was 'as spoilt as a child' and 'so he had better keep that up' despite her having a small inheritance that she could use as her own money. As he works long and irregular hours, often on the weekend, she would justify her spending sprees as revenge for him neglecting her on Saturdays and Sundays, when she was looking after the children singlehanded. She said her way of getting back at him was guilt-free because he denied her weekend trips away.

Looking at this, we see that not only has consumerism become distinct from the need to consume, but feeds emotional needs.

Consumer society – exclusion and inclusion

Clearly one of the successes of consumerism is that it harbours the status quo within the binary of rebellion; individuals are able to feed their desire to be different within the consumerist dream. However there is, then, the potential for this rebellion to be expressed outside of the law, which the riots in London and elsewhere bore witness to. In the project 'Reading the Riots', jointly organised by the Guardian and the London School of Economics and funded by the Joseph Rowntree Foundation[22], their first phase findings, consisting of 270 anonymous interviews (185 in London, 30 in Birmingham, 29 in Manchester, 16 in Liverpool, 7 in Salford and 3 in Nottingham), as well as analysis of 2.5 million riot-related tweets from the University of Manchester, saw a great many respondents admit 'they just wanted free stuff' – particularly branded clothing items.

Truly one of the most interesting aspects of consumer capitalism today is that even subversion is a profitable element. What seemed to characterise the biggest disturbance in Britain for a long time was not despair at financial exclusion per se, but exclusion from consumer society – which should give us pause.

From the records:

> "Interviewees – particularly younger looters – talked about the pressure and 'hunger' for the right 'SIC' brand names. There was a culture of 'wanting SIC stuf', said one 18-year old. "It's like, seen as if you're not wearing, like, and you're poor, no one don't want to be your friend." A 16- year old girl boasted that the next day her room looked like JD Sports –one of the worst hit retail shops, losing £700,000 of stock."

The riots were not politically motivated, but to be sure there was political meaning to address behind them. The evidence suggested by the study of the riots found that rioters were generally poorer than the country at large. Analysis of 1,000 court records shows that 59 per cent of the rioters came from the most deprived 20 per cent of UK areas, while other analyses to come from the Department of Education and the Ministry of Justice note that 64% of riot defendants came from the poorest fifth of areas while only 3 per cent came from the richest.

Since time immemorial, and which accounts for an important aspect of the debate around consumerism, there has been the argument that those with less money should be able to enter into the fold of consumerism as a right to enjoy those same things that the rich enjoy. The disparity in how much more a rich person can afford to enjoy the luxuries of consumerism than of a poorer person. The argument that consumer society should be a luxury afforded to all is one that has been on the table for a long time. Henry Ford and Alfred Sloan were among the first to understand this. As industrialists, it was their realisation that they couldn't simply make products without people buying them. Lots of people. There had to be some popular way in which to develop ways of purchasing. The response was consumer credit.

The growth of consumer credit

The UK, Germany and France represent the countries with the largest national consumer credit markets in the EU. In 1971 there was only one type of credit card in the UK, issued by Barclays. Fast-forward to today and that number is far into the thousands. In that time money owed on credit cards has risen substantially – in 1971 it was £32 million, while in 2009 it was £25 billion.

Attanasio and Weber[23] in their 1994 paper 'The Consumption Boom of the late 1980s' point out that in the UK, in the late 80s, there was an increase in the average propensity to consumer (APC). There has been much speculation over what caused this, which in turn bolstered a consumer boom. While some say it was to do with regulation relaxation, many put it down to an imperfect housing market. But while the authors of the paper agree that household prices were important, that does not explain away the 'surge' of consumption after 1986. Instead they account for it by noting an upward revision in expected labour income, proven by the fact that younger cohorts were the ones who backed the surge. Household savings fell during this period and it seemed that younger people were spending in the present day in the supposed knowledge that their incomes would increase later. Consumers, in other 'consumer booms', have not always been so lucky as to expect higher wage packets.

Raising the old relics of Ford and Sloan, academics Thomas, Oliver and Hand[24] in their paper on consumer credit modelling noted that household debt in the US exceeded $7.2 trillion in the year 2000, which had doubled since 1990 (now, despite shrinking by $126 billion from September 2011 to December 31, Q4 in that year saw total US household debt at $11.53 trillion, according to a Federal Reserve Bank of New York survey). In the UK, in 1993, there were 1,316 million card transactions, of which 3,728 were by credit card. By 2002 plastic usage had outdone cheque usage: 4,814 million transactions were made on card, of which 1,687 were credit card transactions, compared to only 2,393 cheque transactions. The boom time in the 1980s may have been underpinned by the expectation of higher earnings, but to maintain consumption today carries the price of huge debt.

It has always been claimed that the existence of consumer credit is the signpost of a good and healthy economy, in most part because it seems to signal that consumers far and wide, rich and poor, are partaking in consumer capitalism. Certainly, part of the changing logic of capitalism itself has been that it should not be elitist; rather, the propensity to consume should be a privilege enjoyed by the many, not the few. The rise in consumerism, and the return of consumerist principles such as the one that says all should enjoy the fruits of it, might seem noble – and it is not for me here to suggest otherwise. But we ought to dispel the myth that the rise in debt, particularly personal debt, has been a consequence of low-income earners' entry into the consumer capitalist fold. This in turn simply seeks to dignify the opinion that increasingly off-the-scale levels of personal debt, such as the UK is experiencing today, is a subsequent problem of the masses living beyond their means alone. So while it is important to address and understand consumerism and consumer capitalism, we must look at the real factors that feed into high personal debt levels today.

The personal debt context

Levels of personal debt are extremely high in the UK. Total UK personal debt stood at £1.458 trillion at the end of June 2012, a figure which might have been serviceable in better times, but after a recession is only bleak. Projections suggest that the figure is likely to increase to £2.1 trillion by 2015. What did this? As previously discussed, conversations on consumerism often follow the trope that people have been allowed to spend over their means. Nobody is denying this does happen. We talk today of the credit boom, and this was the textbook for people spending over their means. The exploding of the US housing bubble, presided over by Alan Greenspan, showed us to what extent people were able to acquire mortgage loans of several times their annual income. Not only were we spending over our means, we had little choice but to do so.

My primary criticism is that, in spite of the debt landscape, there is a lot more than just overspending that is at fault. The outlook is far more depressing on closer inspection.

Despite the massive expansion in consumer credit that took place during the 1990s, in 2002 over one in five adults, or 7.8 million people, were denied access to mainstream sources of credit. Though the UK as a whole is said to have paid down a good deal of its overall debt in 2011, according to Price Waterhouse Coopers (PwC)[25] each household continues to be saddled with around £7,900 in unsecured debt, making it the most indebted in the world. On top of this, PwC has noticed that there is a rise in the underbanked, with the supply of credit restrained and mainstream lenders being more selective, as well as consumers worrying that their credit scores could be affected as they struggle to cope with challenging economic conditions.

To sit with the figure of 13.5 million Britons living in low-income households, who are disproportionately represented by the underbanked, we find that the UK does not fare well among its European neighbours for basic bank accounts, in spite of recent political efforts. Around 1.75 million UK adults go without a transactional bank account, whereas in France that figure is between 500,000 and 1 million, and in Germany 500,000. In the UK, there are 7.7 million accounts without credit facilities, nearly four times the number of Germany (2 million at the end of 2006) and France (2.1 million in 2008), while 9 million people cannot access credit from mainstream banks in the UK, as opposed to around 2.5 million in Germany and between 2.5 million and 4.1 million in France[26].

Unsurprisingly, UK households borrow around twice as much as France and Germany, with only Cypriots ahead of us in the EU[27].

A 2010, survey of consumer vulnerability, quoted in a report sponsored by Barclays to look at the financial landscape, found that 43 per cent of British households had experienced financial difficulties with their household bills or credit commitments at least sometime in the past 12 months.

'Changing Fortunes' (2011), by Stephen Jenkins, Professor of Economic and Social Policy at the London School of Economics[28], aims to understand poverty and income mobility in recent times, not simply by giving a series of figures showing the amount of poverty and exclusion at any one time, but piecing together this research to come to a more rounded, understanding of its impact. For example, using evidence based on data from the British Household Panel Survey (BHPS) which covered years 1991–2006, we learn that of the people in 1991 who were considered poor, most of them were not considered poor in the subsequent year. In fact, a third of the poor in 1991 were not poor in the subsequent year, but as there was movement toabove the poverty level, there was simultaneous entry into it as well, which meant that the snapshot of poverty in the UK stayed consistent. In short, when looking at poverty in the UK what we see is that there is a proportion of around a fifth who are below the poverty line, but given the level of small-scale dynamics, the proportion of those who are, in their lifetime, affected by poverty, or 'touched' by it, is far higher.

From numbers addressed by the Resolution Foundation, we find also that over a quarter of low earners say that they usually run out of money each month and over a half of low earners report problems with bills and credit commitments. To bolster the financial exclusion that is present here, a report entitled 'Behind the Balance Sheet', by Sophia Parker tells us:

> "Low earning households were much less likely to own insurance to cover unexpected crises, from illness to burglary to job loss – with just 39 per cent of low earners, compared with 58 per cent of higher earners, owning a life insurance policy. Furthermore, low earning households – particularly those under the age of 55 – were much less likely to be saving adequately than higher earners, with 44 per cent of this age group having less than one month's income in the bank, and nearly three quarters having less than two months of income saved."[29]

Figures like these remind us how susceptible many are to taking out emergency loans, not due to overspending, but through being unable to prepare themselves through times of financial 'shocks'. While incredible levels of debt and financial exclusion are a reality, for so many there are no savings for rainy days. A 2011 poverty and social exclusion assessment by the Joseph Rowntree Foundation[30] found that children who are in the poorest fifth of households are around twice as likely to go without essential items as children in households with average incomes. They exemplify the finding that 70 per cent of the poorest children live in households that cannot afford to save £10 a week, or take a week's holiday away from home once a year. Comparable figures for children in households with average incomes are in the mid-thirties. By 2008, the UK's household saving ratio had fallen to the lowest level since the 1950s and household debt had risen to 100 per cent of GDP. 27 per cent of households had no savings and low-income households saved even less, with 41 per cent of those households having no savings.

Wealth redistribution measures

Former chancellor Alistair Darling coyly admitted that many of the policies he presided over were, by any other term, redistribution of UK wealth. Noting that it would not have been politically sensible to admit so at the time, under his tenure the state was redefining the terms of what it could do to solve the problem of poverty. Two of the more popular measures at the time were the Child Trust Fund (CTF) and the Savings Gateway. So wide were their reach that many Tories and Labour supporters alike recognised their merit. They fed in to an international conversation about the future of the welfare state, particularly how it could benefit from asset-based welfare, which is what the two interventions were. They were conceived of in various reports by the Fabian Society and the Institute for Public Policy Research (IPPR) that proposed that every 18-year-old should receive a capital grant from the state, financed from inheritance tax reform. A family received a voucher for £250 or £500 dependent on income and disability status of their child, which they then put into a CTF. If they did not open one in a year, the HMRC opened one automatically. A second voucher would be received by the family when the child reached age 7. Family or friends could put money in up to the amount of £1,200. There was no tax on gains, and the recipient enjoyed three different types of accounts – stakeholder, shares and savings, in addition to ethical and Sharia CTFs.

The official reason for its being killed off was that it would be dishonest for the government to endow children with an asset when public debt was so high. Some who were more cynical of the government's version pointed out that it was an easy cut, and not too politically sensitive, as there were no direct losers to the policy, in that nothing was taken away as such. From August 2010 payments were reduced to £50 and £100 and payments at the age of 7 were stopped completely. By January 2011 all payments were stopped, saving the government £500 million every year. But the argument for it was that it gave people who were previously unable to establish a savings habit a fighting chance.

The same applied to the Savings Gateway, where the government allowed a savings account for low-income earners to add up to £25 a month, which at the end of a two-year period would see the government add 50p in every £1 (One-third of low-income and families identified with extra needs were entitled to extra government contributions, which means accounts received booster payments as intended.)

Dalia Ben-Galim in her paper for the IPPR[31] opined that it was the Liberal Democrats who wanted to get rid of it, while the Tories would probably have halved it. The Lib Dems were concerned that low-income families were not saving enough and that the money for the CTF could be better spent on social mobility elsewhere, for example, through the pupil premium or early years services, and promised to scrap it in their manifesto. Instead of trying to improve upon something that began so well, this represented a desire by the Liberals to just give up. Research has shown that, while not everyone was benefitting from the system, or using it in the correct way, it was addressing a massive deficit in a savings culture for most. While the value of measures such as early years services are beyond doubt, they are not necessarily pitched in this way – what will they be teaching us to do differently?

Ben-Galim hoped that the coalition government would look towards the US and Canada to see what kind of best practice they can glean from there, particularly in a time of sluggish growth. However, now a good way into parliament with the coalition government, we have not yet seen anything that picks up on the sort of culture shift needed – unless, of course, you count David Cameron's urge for all households to 'pay off their debts' as one shift, which Larry Elliot, the *Guardian's* Economics Editor, called at the time "smart politics, but dumb economics".[32]

The real causes of poverty

In 2011, The Human City Institute, a Birmingham-based think-tank, published a report[33] looking at the make-up of 252 people who were tenants of the Trident Group. Of the sample group, some 54 per cent spend more than 10 per cent of their incomes on fuel bills – the official measure of fuel poverty. Nationwide, the figure was around 7.8 million people in 2009, and it is set to rise to 8.5 million by 2016. Professor John Hills said that around 3,000 people died each year as a consequence of fuel poverty, which would increase as energy costs rose. Between 1996 and 2006 fuel poverty had dropped quite substantially, but projections estimate that it will have risen in 2016 to levels not seen since 1996.[34]

Social and financial exclusion, the breaking down of savings initiatives on the excuse that the country cannot afford them anymore, and the rising cost in utilities – these are the things that are likely to make people poor in this country, as opposed to consumerist overspend. Even in the boom years between 1997–2007, barriers to credit were experienced by the most vulnerable in society. With banks lending less, exclusion from these types of financial products is a reality for many more people. Consumers today are avoiding banks at all costs through fear that their credit scores will deteriorate, which means less chance of using them in the future. Unemployment is rising (public sector job losses could be up to 710,000 by 2017, and there is no evidence yet that the private sector will be able to fill in to such a level), the cuts are biting and growth is limp, and yet the cost of living is rising. Further, the cost of raising children is rising dramatically, and people aren't getting much richer.

As Stewart Lansley in his book 'The Cost of Inequality'[35] has written between 1980 and 2007 real wages in UK rose by an annual average of 1.6 per cent, while economic capacity grew by 1.9 per cent. In the mid-2000's real incomes for a large part

of the workforce was at best static and in the two years to 2007
wages barely kept up with inflation, while median incomes
rose by a mere 0.4 per cent per year, representing around £1
a week. The share of the wealth of the bottom 50 per cent has
been shrinking from 10 per cent in the 1980s to six per cent
in 2002, and **real incomes in UK have been near-stagnant
since 2005.**

On the back of this, a new sector, a foreign import from
the US has seen a rise in the UK: offering unsecured loans, no
questions asked, quickly but expensively: it's the payday loan
industry.

CHAPTER 3
LOAN SHARKS

THE LAST CHAPTER described how spending on consumer credit accounted for a large part of economic growth in the years preceding the crisis:

- 1.75 million people do not have access to a transactional bank account;

- 7.7 million accounts are without credit facilities;

- A further 9 million cannot access credit from mainstream banks;

- The UK has worryingly high levels of people who are totally unbanked;

- Credit cards in circulation dropped by 1 million in 2011 and total credit card borrowing dropped by 5 per cent. If, as PwC anticipate in their report 'Precious Plastics', the credit card is going through a mid-life crisis, what is there to pick up where it left off?

The rise in the payday loan industry in the UK has been unprecedented. For such a new phenomenon it has grown to levels other industries can only dream of. It has been helped along by increasing inequality in the UK, by distrust of the banking system, the internet revolution and is guaranteed towering profit margins even when the state of the economy as a whole is in dire straits.

Its origin and growth tells a disturbing story of how little the UK decided it was appropriate to do about the industry, allowing it to flourish even when countries like the US, where experience of the industry goes back many years, had done its best to price out such lenders.

Before discussing the specific origins of the industry, it is necessary to explore the conditions both in the UK and elsewhere that led to the growth of the payday loan market, and other financial products that are often talked about in conjunction with it.

The payday loan market – its origins and growth

As has been discussed in a previous chapter, borrowing money and banking money were once the sole preserve of the wealthy in society, and the working classes had to make do with informal savings clubs or non-bank forms of borrowing.

Provident Financial

The historian Ruth Cherrington remembers her own mother, as well as many others, receiving Provident cheques which could only be spent at certain shops in the local town, usually for school uniforms and other clothes. "The local Provident lady called once a week to collect an installment of repayment and I guess there was some interest added, but the Provident was a respectable company with a long history. Few mothers had enough cash, so this was the only way."

Provident Financial is very much seen by some as a trusted source of credit. Provident, or 'the Provvy' was set up in the 19th century to offer loans to the vast majority who were at that time excluded by banks. Dr Cherrington noted that when she was growing up, the unbanked working class continued to look to Provident; today that is still the case, with growth projections on the rise. The 2011 interim report of the Bradford-based home credit provider reads:

"There will be no change to the cautious stance on extending new credit in recognition of the continuing pressure on consumers' real incomes and remaining uncertainty over the future direction of the employment market."

This was whilst reporting growing earnings in both the home credit arm, operating in the UK and Ireland, and the Vanquis Bank – its 'growing credit care business'– strongly supported by the group's 'excellent capital generation'.

The notion that Provident operates with caution does not sit comfortably with everyone. It has gained a reputation for being the company that really will lend to anybody, whatever the circumstances. In a report by Professor Paul Jones of John Moores University for the Co-operative Bank on access to credit,[36] he quoted one focus group member who told him: "The Provvy's fast cash, reliable and will always say yes", while another one pointed out "there is the Provvy woman, she begged me to take out another loan, she told me that she'd be getting her wages cut if I didn't take out a loan."

The optimism of Peter Crook, chief executive of Provident, is not unfounded. According to the Citizens' Advice Bureau, Provident itself reported a 7 per cent rise in customer numbers to 2.3 million in the first six months of 2010, with profits up 1.7 per cent to £54.1 million. It would be very difficult not to remember, while looking at Peter Crook's optimism, something he said in 2010 while assessing the effect of George Osborne's Spending Review of October, 2010: "We may well see a growth in our target audience." Writing for the *Guardian*, Faisal Rahman, Managing Director of Fair Finance, pointed out,[37] with his tongue firmly in his cheek, that "In a week of unrelenting bad news about cuts in public sector spending, it's good that [Peter Crook can] see the silver lining."

Pointing out the pressure on consumers' incomes and uncertainty over jobs, as Crook does in his report, is another reoccurring theme, namely that in order to justify the product

Provident is selling, they must relay the problems of the wider economic landscape. Assessing the many interviews with people who have resorted to taking out credit with Provident, it is no wonder that Peter Crook is so keen to embrace how society has failed the most vulnerable. In a report by Policis,[38] viewed by some as largely sympathetic to the home credit and payday lending industry, it was pointed out that, of the sample of people they interviewed, many were of the opinion that borrowing was the only way to manage cash shortfalls. One interviewee told them: "At the end of the day, if it wasn't for Provident, we wouldn't have anything", while another said: "If it wasn't for the Provident, I'd either have to go without or go shop-lifting or buying stuff off the shop-lifters because I wouldn't be able to buy clothes or trainers at normal prices." Whether it is an erroneous perception by the interviewee that borrowing home credit is their only alternative, or whether this is precisely the case, Provident is able to use this towards a moral high ground and excuse the fact that they charge large sums for the product they sell.

As Henry Palmer and Pat Conaty write in their 2003 report for the New Economics Foundation 'Profiting from Poverty',[39] one Provident client borrowed £400 over 53 weeks, repaying a total of £636 – an APR of 164 per cent. All the while Provident can say, mostly to uncritical ears, that if it did not provide individuals with a loan, then there would be plenty of scope for illegal alternatives to move in.

Cost vs. convenience

In 2009 the then Shadow Housing Minister Grant Shapps opined that the lack of competition in the home credit market means that exorbitant rates of interest can be explained by the fact that only very few businesses control the market. As Shapps put it, 90 per cent of the home credit market is dominated by just six companies.[40] By changing the life and size of their average loan from 1996 to 2002, Provident alone was able to increase the revenue it earned on every £1 from 47.7p to 52.6p.

Veronika Thiel, writing on doorstep lending for the New Economics Foundation,[41] found that the typical amount loaned by a home credit provider is around £200 but could be anything between £50 and £500, with average APRs of 150 per cent paid back over a period of between 30 and 50 weeks. Other doorstep lenders such as Morses or S & U charge similar rates, where a loan of £485 over 75 weeks on an average APR of 160 per cent could end up costing £900. As Stella Creasy MP said: "It is very expensive in this country to be poor."

While home credit products seem outrageously expensive, there are clearly elements that appeal, such as the convenience of receiving it from home. A survey by the Office of Fair Trading in 2010 found that users of home credit are:

- Substantially overrepresented in lower social classes;

- Have markedly lower income;

- Have lower levels of final educational achievement;

- A much higher proportion of single parents; and

- Substantially more likely to be unemployed or not in paid employment.

It is not surprising to learn that mainstream credit is often off the cards. But research also suggests that there is a level of best practice attached to the home credit industry that could be put to better use. In Karen Rowlingson's monograph on the home credit industry 'Moneylenders and their Customers'[42] she evaluates the relationship of lenders with their customers. Rowlingson points out three main dimensions:

1) The personal level which varies in levels of formality from business-like and formal to friendly and informal;
2) The balance of power between lenders and customers; and

3) The 'underlying nature of the relationship' which can range
    from exploitative to supportive.

Clearly what can be drawn from this is the potential to have
a service that provides the best elements and leaves the negative bits aside.

Taking note of the convenience of home credit, a Joseph
Rowntree Foundation, (2009), published a report assessing whether there could be scope for a not-for-profit home
credit provider – taking the best from the industry and seeing
whether it could be achieved at a price that doesn't exploit the
customer.[43] The study concluded that even without profit, at
a break-even rate, 129 per cent APR was going to be typical
on a loan of £288 over an average 56-week loan, assuming an
investment of £18 million with the intention of becoming cash-
positive, operating without further investment, after five years.
That investment, incorporated into the funding of a community lender, social enterprise or credit union is not unrealistic,
but is by no means cheap. Having said this, because the market
has few operators, and with other credit options being available
such as payday loans on the high street, prices will only increase
– which means the disparity between for profit and not-for-
profit prices will become wider. A Competition Commission
inquiry, cited by the Joseph Rowntree Foundation, noted that
the low number of home credit lenders has led to higher costs,
averaging at approximately £7 more per £100 borrowed than
could have been expected 'in a market in which competition
ensured prices reflected only the costs of provision'.

Those who use home credit for convenience may have to
accept that they bear the brunt of additional costs that reflect
a high break-even rate, even if the business is not-for-profit, or
from a credit union (which would immediately find this service
difficult given their legal obligation to an APR cap of 26.8 per
cent). The thing that should give us pause here is what is meant
by Peter Crook when he says that due to the highly concerning

economic outlook, his company may see a growth in its target audience as they find themselves with fewer options – and indeed looking at later reports on the growth of Provident, his assumption has clearly come true. Finding ways to ensure people are not reduced to accepting in hard times financial products that they cannot afford and that are expensive should really be the main concern here.

Pawnbrokers

Along with home credit, another service that has served customers who themselves have few options elsewhere are pawnbrokers.

Edward Lewis in his 1992 work 'An Introduction to Credit Scoring'[44] pointed out that pawnbroking has been around for the last 750 years, dating back to the usurers of the Middle Ages. As has already been discussed, back in the 1800s pawnbrokers were an every day part of many the lives of many families, pawning off clothes on Monday, using the money in the week and buying back the clothes at the weekend for a special Saturday night or Sunday religious event. In early 2012 the number of pawnbroker shops in the UK had grown by 56 per cent to 1,412 since 2009. On high streets they can often be found in the same shops that offer short-term cash loans at expensive rates of interest, or cheque cashing for high fees. According to the *Guardian*, in February 2012 "Pawnbrokers' investors, too, have thrived through the economic slowdown. Albemarle & Bond shares, 218p just before the 2008 banking crisis, now change hands at some 340p. Rival Harvey & Thompson has seen its shares climb from 175p to 336p over the same period."[45]

Unlike with the home credit product, pawnbrokers usually offer loans against household items as security, and research by the New Local Government Network found that they are used by about 2 per cent of the very poorest quintile of the population.[46]

In this sense, they are comparably closer to logbook loans, where a loan is offered against the value of a car or motorbike, giving the lender the right to that vehicle if the loan is not paid back (though usually this type of loan is costlier in interest for higher amounts of money).

It has been subject to very little research considering what a focal part it has played in the sub-prime market for so long. A rare full-length report on the subject published in 2010, with research carried out by the Personal Finance Research Centre (PFRC) at the University of Bristol, noted that when the National Pawnbrokers Association was founded in 1892 there were around 900 outlets in the UK.[47] We know that the *Pawnbroker's Gazette* was established in 1838, so the industry has definitely had a long lifespan. Whereas back then it was a vital part of the life of a working class family who generally had no access to bank accounts, nowadays the customer profile tends to be mainly female with an average age of 39, living with families with dependent children. Incomes tend to be low (below £300 a week) and 53 per cent live in households where nobody is at work.

The most commonly heard reason for using a pawnbroker was to pay household bills. With 40 per cent of users holding only a basic bank account compared with the national rate of 5 per cent, most felt they had very few other options and payday loans were cited frequently as being the only other option they had. The average loan from a pawnbroker was around £90, a loan agreement was for a minimum of six months after which the pawned item can be sold off. Commonly pledged items were rings, gold items, necklaces and bracelets. 54 per cent of customers were able to receive their items back after this time, according to the sample researched by the PFRC.

Of the pawnbrokers in the UK, Cash Converters enjoys the largest market share. The company originated in Australia in 1984, growing in the UK to 90 franchises in 2002, a figure that has now grown to 200 according its website, with plans for 50 new stores. As with home credit, the existence of the product relies on poor economic conditions to justify itself. Barry Stevenson, the chief executive of Albemarle & Bond, said in response to news that the industry he works in was growing rapidly again: "There's hardly any bureaucracy and no intrusive checks; we treat people like human beings, unlike a lot of banks." (he also told *The Times* that 2012 marked the beginning of the "age of the pawnbroker").

There can be no denying that the banks deserve their bashing, but that the pawnbroking industry today can use the banking sector as a benchmark to hide behind while enjoying roaring trade from people feeling desperate enough to have to part with their possessions to get by, should surely make us uncomfortable – particularly when you consider the prices. Featured in Paul Jones' research on access to credit is an example of the type of prices we are looking at here: "Pledge an item of jewellery against a £200 loan at Miltons, St John's Centre, Liverpool, and reclaim it for £220 eight weeks later (APR 85.8 per cent)".

High street chains

However exploitative, these prices can often seem timid in comparison to other high street chains such as BrightHouse, formerly known as Crazy George's, which can be found setting up shop in working class neighbourhoods (in Polly Toynbee's book *'Hard Work'*[48] she notes that "Wherever there is a Starbucks, a Waterstone's, a Jigsaw or a Habitat you can bet there isn't a Crazy George's nearby"). One of the major concerns about BrightHouse is the way in which it presents its prices. While they charge reasonably competitive levels of APR of around 29 per cent, the total APR including the 'optional cover' was much higher (while one company director, quoted by the NEF in one of its reports, did insist it was optional, noted that 90 per cent of customers took it out because of previous experience with credit agreements). The interest on a gas cooker, say, at £386.86 would cost £3.57 a week for 156 weeks at 29.9 per cent, totalling £556.92. But with the 'optional cover' that price is pushed up to £856.44. BrightHouse product prices are above the market rate, so the true cost is even higher.

After it was revealed that BrightHouse was charging above the odds for goods, *The Sun* newspaper in 2009 reported that: "After several BrightHouse products were shown to be cheaper in Harrods, the company said they didn't consider Harrods to be a competitor. The fact it was more than 10 miles away meant its pledge to beat rivals on price didn't apply".[49]

To justify their prices, companies such as BrightHouse might say they deal with a riskier type of customer, but without doubt they find it profitable to do so, at the expense of the most vulnerable in society – who ironically pay more for the pleasure of being vulnerable. Caversham Finance Limited, previously a subsidiary of Thorn Group plc, was taken private in September 1998 in a deal arranged and financed by the Principal Finance Group of Nomura (now reconstructed as Terra Firma Capital Partners). The company was bought by Vision Capital in July 2007, and of all the portfolio of investments for Vision Capital, BrightHouse is one of their key players with revenues of £229 million – beaten only by investments in Bormioli Rocco (€531 million – around £449 million) and Portman Travel (around £300 million). To be sure, BrightHouse does not struggle to provide its expensive service.

Regulating cash lending

How these products survive has a lot to do with the regulatory system in the UK. In the years running up to 1974, cash lending was regulated by the 1948 Moneylenders Act, which capped interest rates at 48 per cent. But its successor legislation the Consumer Credit Act, which created a framework for the regulation of all types of consumer credit, abandoned the interest rate ceiling, leaving the onus on the courts to decide whether a credit agreement was 'grossly exorbitant' and the result of 'fair dealing'. Given that so few working class consumers brought such cases to the courts, very little was done. Consequently, the door was opened for high-cost products to be levelled at the most vulnerable at a time when economic conditions did little to favour them.

A common get-out is that banks are failing low income families, and while this is true, as will be discussed later, this often provides a useful mask for exploitative business practices, rather than excuses them.

The US experience

While the looseness of the regulatory system in the UK helped create the conditions for a widening of the short-term – or payday – lending industry, it is no coincidence that American-backed companies, new to UK, were popping up at the same time as some US states were kicking them out or better defining their regulations over them. Michael Stegman, writing in 2007,[50] on the US market said: "Virtually no payday loan outlets [which bore resemblance to 'salary buyers' who would buy, at a discounted price, a borrower's next wage packet] existed 15 years ago". Now at least 5 per cent of all US citizens have taken out such a loan.

According to an influential report by Flannery and Samolyk in 2005[51], the payday lending industry originated in a shadow form, in the US in the early 1980s. It was largely felt to be the outcome of the Depository Institutions Deregulation and Monetary Control Act in 1980, which was a reaction by the federal government to the rise in inflation, effectively overriding all existing state and local usury laws, giving way to the elimination of interest rate limits.

In the American states where usury was made illegal or payday lending better regulated, lenders would still lend, but operate as best they could within the new rules. Notably, in 1978, there was the case of the *Marquette National Bank of Minneapolis* vs. *First of Omaha Service Corp.*, a Supreme Court decision ruled that state anti-usury laws could not enforce against nationally chartered banks in other states. This decision upheld the constitutionality of the National Bank Act, permitting chartered banks to charge their highest home-state interest rates in any state in which they operated. Subsequently, as payday lenders were partnering with banks and seeing their product repackaged as 'bank loans', some lenders were setting up shop in states where usury laws were more relaxed and lending to people in states where usury laws were tighter, but effectively overridden.

Another point to note is that many early US payday products were simply cheque cashing, which had no interest attached to them, only fees. The concerned states soon created separate, specific, legislation as these products were not captured within the usury framework developed.

The US regulatory architecture has squeezed many payday lenders out of the market, meaning they would inevitably seek home elsewhere. While some US states restrict payday loans to 25 per cent of income, 15 states in the US have banned payday loans altogether or levelled a low interest rate cap at them, driving some lenders out of business. In Arizona, California, Colorado, and Florida there exists a restriction on the number of loans one person can take out at any one time to one, Indiana at two. Alabama restricts rollovers to one, Alaska two, while Illinois, Kentucky, and Louisiana prohibit rollovers entirely. Additionally, there is a federal cap for lenders on rates for military personnel at 36 per cent.

The industry was exported to the UK in the 1990s where The Money Shop, a payday lender owned by US company Dollar Financial Corp, expanded from having one shop in 1992 dealing primarily with cheque cashing, to 273 stores and 64 franchises across the UK in 2009. Today five of the seven biggest payday loan companies in the UK are owned or controlled by a US company. An article in the *Financial Times* in December 2011 ('Payday sector in search of new frontier'[52]) showed the extent to which payday loan migration was still occurring from the states, reporting on four American representatives of the business Speedy Cash which came to London looking for places they could set up shop, now that their hometowns were accusing them of exploiting the desperate in recessionary times. They searched high and low in places such as Barking, Ilford, Kilburn and Wood Green: "parts of the city most visitors would only end up in by mistake ... anywhere that wasn't Westminster, Chelsea or Richmond".

Market growth

For these businesses now could not be a better time to tap into the UK market. Tim Harford repeated the claim in his article, asking whether the industry was really so immoral,[53] noting that payday lending was up from £100 million in 2004 to £1.7 billion in 2010. Modest, he argued, compared with over £55 billion of outstanding credit card debt or more than £200 billion of consumer credit; but for a relatively new product that is having another growth spurt since the financial crash of 2007-8, it is considerable. Looked at from the market share viewpoint is one thing, but looked at another way, in 2007 the market had grown from £100 million to £500 million, and in 2010 had increased some 200 per cent. If we look at where these loans are going, we see that much of it is concentrated to the very vulnerable who are using what they can borrow to pay bills or buy food. Compared to the rest of Europe, payday loans are most prevalent in the UK, followed behind by the Netherlands and Latvia, and companies such as The Money Shop and QuickQuid are household names.

Joanna Elson, chief executive of the Money Advice Trust, pointed out at the start of 2012 that the growth of payday lending had caused an increase in the number of calls to its debt counselling service, saying: "Just two years ago National Debtline was receiving around 150 calls per month from people with payday loans – that figure has now ballooned to 1,100."

Payday players

In a short time, the payday loan industry has been very successful in making its presence known. Merely saying how little of the overall market share it occupies right now neglects to contextualise where it was before the crash and before the migration of American businesses, which were either moved on or took it upon themselves to go before the authorities had the chance to move them. From information collated in 2010 by statutory consumer organisation Consumer Focus, operating in the UK are: Dollar Financial Corp (which, under its belt, includes The MoneyShop and online provider Express Finance (Bromley) Ltd); MEM Consumer Finance (which is the second largest market player after Dollar Financial Corp, the largest internet provider, and trades as MonthEnd Money, Payday Now, PayDay UK, PaydayStore, Quicksilver and Payday Loans); Cheque Centres, CashEuronet UK LLC (which trades as QuickQuid); Albemarle & Bond Holdings PLC (including Herbert Brown & Son); H & T Pawnbrokers; and National Cash Advances. With new ventures emerging all the time it is very difficult to keep track of what these organisations are trading under from one day to the next, what new online businesses have appeared and what start-ups have taken advantage of the loosely regulated market.

Studies, particularly from the US (where far more work has been carried out on the effects of payday loans), suggest, unsurprisingly, that credit like this is often detrimental to personal finances in the long term. So while lenders themselves may cling to the excuse that they are filling in a void, the onus is upon the regulatory system in the UK to make sure that void is filled with products, interventions and, importantly, advice that can be a help, rather than a hindrance to individuals who struggle to get to payday. Returning to Stegman's 2007 report, he notes that payday lending stores in the US are concentrated in low income neighbourhoods and that levels of repeat borrowing demonstrate that "some families with fragile finances can become addicted to payday loans".

The origins and growth of the industry in the UK show the same signs. The question should also be raised why banks have chosen to "outsource", in the words of Veronika Thiel, the subprime lending market elsewhere.

Who are payday loans for? Do they justify their prices?

The Consumer Finance Association (CFA), a trade body for the payday lending industry, has a pamphlet on its website offering five tips for borrowers:

1. That they must be in work and have a bank account;
2. That they should only consider their loan short term;
3. That they should be in full understanding of what is to be paid back;
4. That they should understand what repayment costs there will be if the loans are not paid back on time;
5. That they should confirm for themselves that the place they are borrowing from is reputable.

In another pamphlet the CFA points out that 50 per cent of payday borrowers' incomes are in excess of £19,200 per annum and 75 per cent earn over £15,000. Consumer Focus find similar, saying that payday lending customers tend to be concentrated in the range below median income but generally above the lowest bands, while independent consultancy Policis, on behalf of Friends Provident Foundation, find that one in ten UK payday loan customers have incomes of less than £11,100 per year. Moreover, 67 per cent of users have incomes of under £25,000 per annum, whereas in the US that is 75 per cent, where it is also notable that adults without bank accounts are the ones using payday loans.

Sally Chicken, the volunteer director of Ipswich and Suffolk Credit Union provided an example of 'Julieta', a person on a low wage, who found it impossible to get to the end of the week without falling short, decided to take out a short-term loan, and struggled to get back in the black. Sally told me:

> "She took a payday loan of £200 on a Tuesday, and repaid the loan on the same Friday, plus £60 interest. Her pay packet was £290 after tax. So of course she didn't have enough money left to last until next payday so she took another loan from the same payday company a few days later, also repaying it on the Friday with another £60 interest. Her bank statement showed her doing this every week for a month."

Without intervention, it is possible that Julieta could have been stuck in a potentially unmanageable long-term debt cycle. Sally concluded:

> "Our Loan Officer is now keeping a file when she sees these examples."

But does simply looking at how much borrowers earn give us the full story?

Types of payday user

In the Consumer Focus report 'Keeping the Plates Spinning'[54] they pinpoint the three types of payday user:

- Those who had a long-term negative experience from their loan;

- Those who had a mixed short-term experience; and

- Those who had a short-term positive experience.

Those who had a long-term negative experience tended to take out loans and defer payments, thereby extending the life – and repayments – of the loan. They were often lower income earners, had poor credit ratings, viewed short-term finance solutions as the only way of getting extra money, had previous negative experiences with mainstream forms of credit and felt initially positive about the relative lack of enquiry about a loan than would otherwise be experienced trying to take a personal loan out from a bank.

The short-term mixed experience group, on the other hand, had typically taken only one loan out in the last 12 months, had managed to pay it back on time, but still had reservations about it. This type of borrower also tended to have a low income, few savings, some with existing debts, and the reason they needed a loan was due to a small financial shock such as a later than anticipated pay day or unexpected utility bill. Along with expecting banks to turn them away, they also did not want to even deal with banks, as they felt poorly treated during previous meetings.

The short-term positive experience was as to be expected, using the loan as a one-off, paid back in the allocated time frame and benefitting from the relative anonymity of the transaction. This type of borrower also had few savings, but unlike the others, chose to use this type of loan so as not to impact negatively upon getting a larger loan at another time.

It should be noted that the OFT High Cost Credit Review found that nearly 30 per cent of loans in the UK are not repaid on the initially agreed repayment date of within 30 days/next payday and 10 per cent of payday loans go beyond 90 days. Common to all types was a low income, distrust in banks and little by way of savings, but they differed in terms of how limited they considered their options to be – reliant on anecdote, but a far more nuanced characterisation than just income bracket.

What remains interesting here is to understand the borrower's relationship with banks. Many people find themselves without access to credit facilities at a time when it is largely relied upon by many to be additional to wages. Without it, a lot of people would struggle to maintain the same sort of lifestyle on just their own wages alone, and indeed many of those would have to top-up via alternative means of credit. Individuals who are not considered 'creditworthy' – many of the most vulnerable in society – tend to pay the highest costs for credit, which as Veronika Thiel in her report 'Doorstep Robbery' concludes is: "Something that seems to be accepted [but demonstrates] a social injustice."

A joint report by the PFRC and the Money Advice Trust, which benefitted from qualitative interviews with 30 credit users on low and middle incomes in the summer of 2011,[55] noted that within both those income groups, the strain of reining-in spending but realising the cost of living was rising could be too much to cope with. The conclusion some are left with is that it won't necessarily just be lower income users who will have a bad time with payday loans, but users earning closer to median income also. This group may rely on short-term loans to maintain a decent standard of living, comparable to how some lived during what has become known as the credit boom of the late 1990s and early to mid-noughties (where standards of living were raised, yet wages remained largely stagnant, filled in mainly by ease of credit use).

On top of this, the charity Shelter warned in early 2012 that nearly seven million people in Britain are at risk of 'debt spiralling'[56] through a combination of credit cards, overdrafts and payday loans.

In response to my question on what factors are at play when individuals take out high cost loans, David Rodger, the Managing Director of the Debt Advice Foundation, told me: "We always ask [people who want their support] if they have been to talk to their bank, and as often as not they haven't."

The reason, David explains, is very telling indeed:

> "Banks are seen as intimidating, you have to go in and sit down and talk to someone who you think is going to be critical and judgmental. If people have significant debt problems they tend to assume that the bank won't help."

This, again, provides another excuse with which payday lenders level today justify their product.

What loans are used to fund

Another important element is the kind of things people take out these loans for, and whether it is for things that could have otherwise been settled by a better banking arrangement (such as access to an authorised overdraft) or another arrangement such as a crisis loan by the government. Damon Gibbons of the Centre for Responsible Credit told me that, unlike in the US, the UK has not benefitted from "rigorous study of the long term effects of a payday loan on living standards and essential budgets". He continued: "People cut down on food, heating, may not pay council tax and end up defaulting on other demands. Is it short term or does it have a causal link that hasn't been picked up?"

Gibbons' research tallies with other studies showing that these loans are being taken out to cover basics, not generally to top-up an exuberant lifestyle, as some would have you believe. Ian Murray MP, the Shadow Minister for Employment

Relations, Consumer and Postal Affairs told me that it would not be in his interest to, as he put it, "shut down the legal guys" – even though what their service provided was for people to resolve things many of us take for granted such as paying all our bills. While using legal mechanisms to price out this type of credit entirely would be wrong, exposing people who would have far fewer legal options, it certainly does show that, as it stands, the law is not fit for purpose.

The insolvency experts at R3, in their snapshot on personal debt in November 2011[57] noted that nearly half of those who took out a payday loan (in their research sample) thought, in hindsight, that it had made their financial situation worse (48 per cent), and a significant majority regret taking on a payday loan at all (60 per cent). When I raised the point with Frances Coulson, the President of R3, that legal payday lenders will argue their product is merely filling in where banks fail and illegal loan sharks prey, Coulson replied: "They are certainly filling a market, yes – R3's latest research found that 68 per cent of those sampled who took out a payday loan did so because they couldn't get credit anywhere else." What this should tell us, Coulson said, was that "probably every other type of lender has turned them down, including the banks, and indicates it might be time to take professional advice rather than seeking further credit." Undeniably true, and the lender should – and in fact is legally obliged to – hold some of the responsibility here, too. Sadly, what they are not yet legally obliged to do is signpost free debt advice and clearly signal that their product may not be the cheapest available to the potential borrower.

Are the charges justifiable?

One of the more important debates to be had about the payday loan industry is whether the price charged is justified. One of the things often picked up in the mainstream press is the high APR (annual percentage rate) of the loans. Some industry representatives say the figures, that can often spin off to thousands of per cent, distort the real price attached to a loan that is designed to be short-term, as by definition APR is calculated on a loan duration of a year. If the life span of a loan is, say, 31 days, then looking at the APR alone would tell you very little about the total cost of that loan to the borrower, which will obviously be significantly less than if that loan was live for a year. As the Centre for Responsible Credit put it:

> "APR is an annualised compounded rate and is bound to be higher when tagged to shorter term loans – so is not the best marker to judge how expensive the cost of the total loan will be'. But though the total cost will be significantly less, does it still represent a 'justified' amount?"

Payday lenders finance the main share of their business from internal resources, and if they use bank finance it is typical that 20 per cent of loans must be financed from internal resources. Thus the impetus is for lenders not to be stung by non-payment, though this does not rule out making money from rollover loans. In their 2011 exposure piece on the payday loan industry, the consumer organisation Which? pointed out:

> "Many payday lenders claim that they don't charge interest on interest. Before a loan is rolled over, the previous month's interest has to be paid off. However, consumers can easily apply to two payday lenders in alternate months, using one loan to repay the other, including the accrued interest. By telling customers that their future loans are pre-approved and bigger each month, lenders are effectively building long-term borrowing with compound interest into their lending structure."

How a payday lender works is not complex. Customers sold loans on the high street usually receive cash on site, repaying using a post-dated cheque that is left behind at the time the loan is taken out. Online operations involve money being transferred electronically to the customer's bank account and repayment being taken electronically, either by debit card or direct debit. While this may be straightforward, how companies draw a maximum profit may be slightly counter-intuitive, and at odds with why many worry about them (namely high APR). For example, the costs associated with loans of, say, £200 are the same with loans of £750 – making excessive profit margins on very small loans is tough. On high fixed cost loans, profit is usually by way of the vast amount of loans sold, not the amount of the individual loan itself. The incentive therefore is not to sell a single loan of £1,000, but to sell a loan to a person who will borrow week after week.

One of the questions Flannery and Samolyk[58] ask in their paper is if payday lenders can survive if they provide only 'occasional' credit – which many of them say is their only remit. In other words, could the industry survive if there were fewer high-frequency borrowers? The answer is that they might be able to, but only just. But its long-term scale would be far smaller. To put it another way, for a lender to be completely responsible in their lending, they would have to forego profit maximisation and reduce the lifespan of their business. We have to trust that the industry operates towards an often self-defeating ethical business model that puts its customers before itself. An extremely big ask.

There are price differences in online lenders and those with a shop front which must be taken into consideration. The 'Keeping the Plates Spinning' report asserts, for example, that an online loan can level a typical added rate of £25-£30 for every £100 borrowed, whereas on the high street it is £13-£18 for every £100 borrowed. Matthew Fulton, a key figure in the End the Legal Loansharking campaign initiated by think tank Compass, reports that, from his research, an internet company's break-even point is at around 70 per cent APR. Those payday lenders with a shop front can average at 130-40 per cent depending on the types of scheme and duration. Though we can expect companies to be a bit more risk averse when it comes to pricing in the potential for default, one would expect, given normal market rules, that with so many operators rates would be around this break-even point, not way in excess of it, which is often the case. Online payday lender Ferratum, for example, has a representative APR of 3113 per cent on the assumption that £100 will be borrowed over 30 days.

Claude Saumaise, the 16th century Dutch Calvinist, once said: "Moneylending [is] a business like any other, and like other businesses [is] entitled to charge a market price... If the number of usurers multiplies, the price of money or interest will be driven down by the competition". This fantasy, unfortunately, is still believed by some.

Comparison with bank charges

In the previously mentioned Which? report it is noted that payday lenders often dishonestly compare the price of their product to an unauthorised overdraft so as to make their prices seem better for the customer, and indeed, nine times out of ten it is much cheaper. While payday loan companies (measured on biggest online payday lenders by 12-week UK Google clickthrough rate for the search term 'payday loan') Quick Payday and QuickQuid charge between £20 and £30 for £100 borrowed, and Payday Bank, Payday Kong and Payday UK charge £25, the Co-op bank and Nationwide charge around £21 for an unauthorised overdraft of the same amount, First Direct charge £25, HSBC £26.50, Lloyds TSB £81.46, Barclays £110, Santander £125, Halifax/Bank of Scotland £150 and Natwest/ Royal Bank of Scotland £186 – shocking amounts.

The obvious conclusion is that if one has access to an authorised overdraft this is far cheaper. The prices involved tell their own story: for First Direct there is no charge at all, for the Co-op bank it is £1.35, Nationwide £1.61, Barclays Bank £1.64, Natwest/Royal Bank of Scotland £1.69, HSBC £1.69

(a price which does increase by £25 if not the first overdraft in six months), Santander £5 (50p per day, capped at £5 per month), Lloyds £6.61 and Halifax/Bank of Scotland £26. The problem, however, is quite obvious – that is, such facilities are not available to everyone, particularly among those characterised by banks as risky and sub-prime.

In Paul Jones' work on access to credit, one of the focus group participants put the problem succinctly: "The majority of people around here [Norris Green, large housing estate and council ward in Liverpool] don't deal with banks, they are not for us."

One of the many questions that are raised when talking about the rise in payday lenders, both online and offline, is that banks are allowing this industry to flourish almost without competition. Surely banks should be providing a challenge? There is obviously money to be made here and the economic conditions mean that the product is in high demand. Surely it is not because banks are so risk-averse? Yes, a lot changed after the credit crunch, but city bonus pools returned to pre-crash levels in 2010, while the average pay for chief executives of Britain's largest 100 companies rose by 55 per cent in the first six months of that same year. As Veronika Thiel told me: "Banks in other countries have overdrafts for low income people – banks in the UK aren't going to go under because they're lending out £500 for emergencies."

Tim Harford opined that banks do in fact compete in this market via unauthorised overdrafts. This does not apply to the unbanked, or those with basic accounts or other accounts which do not allow such functions. Damon Gibbons at the Centre for Responsible Credit has his own ideas as to why mainstream banks do not get involved in the payday lenders' target market:

> "The reason is reputational, especially when mainstream banks have got to keep up appearances for the middle class market. With them returns are higher, and there is no

cross-subsidy for lower risk consumers not subsidising the high risk consumer ... though the question is still out as to whether banks *are* expanding in payday funding. Some banks have back-office ties to payday lenders."

The implication therefore being that banks avoiding directly getting their hands dirty, enjoying returns on back-office investments, and keeping their desired image intact – or as far as is possible after the crash.

However, not everybody benefits.

Case study: the story of Steve Perry

There are going to be very few occasions when taking a payday loan will benefit one's personal finances. If your car breaks down before an important meeting for a lucrative contract, and it's the end of the month and the bank won't lend you a little bit until your pay packet comes in, then perhaps, all other options having been exhausted, the speed will come in handy. There are on the other hand times when things work out extremely badly. *The Sun* newspaper ran a story in January 2012 interviewing a woman called Nicky Belgrove[59] who had borrowed £550 from three payday lenders in 2008-9, struggled with repayments and ended up paying back over £3,000 over the course of four months. Examples like these are too frequent, but are rarely discussed by payday lenders themselves.

I had the opportunity to speak to Steve Perry, who had previously been a user of payday loans. He told me that in the space of two years, one loan turned into 64. A few hundred pounds soon turned into £7,000-worth of 'dead money' and total repayments of £22,000. Having taken out a loan to get to the end of the month which he found himself unable to pay back in full, he realised his only option, too worried to ask others around him, was to take out another loan to pay back the first. Payday UK wanted £75 at the end of the month of June 2009, £375 10 days later, or at the very least another £75 to keep them sweet. Steve had taken on a new job and lost income between jobs, which is why he took out the modest loan, which soon escalated into unmanageable level.

By July 13 Steve had taken out the crucial second loan from Payday Express, and after a few months found himself owing £575, after borrowing £460 altogether. By this time he had already paid back £190 in interest. Another loan was taken on August 12 for £260 simply to service his existing debts; four weeks later he was able to pay back £260 to the first loan in August, £75 to Payday UK and £40 to Payday Express. At one point during 2010 his outgoings for debt was £850 per month on a wage of £1,100 per month. This wage is much higher than the lowest wage payday lenders say they will lend to someone on – which is around £750 per month – but in not taking into consideration how much a person's outgoings are highlights a crucial flaw in assessing somebody on income alone, for which we must question how responsible a lender is.

In order to eat he became acquainted with a company called Txtloan, then Lending Stream, and then QuickQuid. He pleaded with the companies he was in trouble with by requesting better suited debt management plans, before the internal debt collections company Keyes Whitlock and Co, the internal debt collections company within MEM Consumer Finance Ltd, which trades as Payday UK, emailed Steve to say since no suitable repayment plan had been set up, his debt was to be dealt with by them.

It got worse before it got better.

There was a loan to cover Christmas that year, a loan from SafeLoan and Wageday Advance just to cover the one from Uncle Buck. The total cost of borrowing for Steve over 21 months was £14,886. He repaid a total of £21,707.49 with interest of £6,821.49. When things had started to settle, he said that he sent his own personal report to John Lamidey, the chief executive of the CFA, but he received no reply.

Steve is very forward with what he wants to see happen to the payday loan industry. Here is what he thinks should be the appropriate course of action on regulating the industry:

> "Ban rollover loans altogether, put in place much more stringent affordability tests, real time credit checks, limit the number of loans taken per year by having cooling-off periods after repayment, introduce a complete overhaul of the advertising rules and prevent targeting the vulnerable."

He was acutely aware of the effect this would have on payday lenders. He went on, "Many, including myself, believe this action would put the majority of the industry out of business because it contradicts their business models. So be it."

Steve has since written a book about his experience, or what he calls his "18 months of torture, over 60 individual payday loans from a dozen companies", writes a blog called Say No to Pay Day Loans[60] and spends a good deal of time writing to the OFT. Unsurprising, really.

The press and the payday lenders

Good or bad press with UK news institutions can often make or break a reputation – politicians fear it, celebrities court it and everyone else can hardly get enough of it. It is testament to the strength of the payday loan market, and the desperation that forces people to their services, that in spite of very active and targeted press campaigns against the industry, it continues to thrive.

Since the beginning of Stella Creasy's campaigns against high cost lenders, and the work of all involved in the End the Legal Loansharking campaign, there is hardly a week goes by without a news article discouraging their use. And with increased attention from journalists comes more scoops on wrongdoing, not to mention how far this can often be fed off the OFT's decision to step up its regulation of the market.

Articles or commentary on the benefits of payday lenders tend to be delivered by economists who are concerned that there is little else available for low-income families. Tim Harford's aforementioned article is one example. But seldom does an article sing the praises on the industry's merit alone. It is usually peppered with an oppositional stance towards UK banks, particularly after high-profile bailouts. Generally, it is accepted by the mainstream press in the UK that the payday lending industry is exploitative of the vulnerable and that they are lucky to have found themselves the opportunity to seek legitimacy through their credit licences. It is interesting to see how some newspapers have worked it into their agenda, and how it reflects their readership.

In 2011 the *Daily Telegraph* ran an article pointing out that legal loan sharks were targeting the military,[61] citing an advert on the website of lender QuickQuid which reads: "You provide security and protection for your country – shouldn't your armour against financial problems include access to military loans when you need them?"

Other publications have been equally as scathing. In 2010 the *Financial Times* warned that "About 1m resort to payday loans",[62] while another points out that "The crisis boosts growth in payday loans".[63] Not simply writing to complain, but to inform, the *FT* published an article saying "Credit unions able to compete".[64] And it is not just the broadsheets. The *Daily Mail* in March 2012 wrote "Britain has become 'wild west' for payday loan lenders."[65] A month before that the *Mail* found that "Pay-day loans used to fund plastic surgery: Website deals linked to good looks".[66] For the FeMail section of the *Daily Mail's* website, one story carried the heading: "How women are being seduced into debt by payday parasites: 'Instant' cash firms with interest rates as high as 16,000% are ruining lives."[67]

The most rigorous of all the tabloid papers is the *Daily Mirror*. Supporters of the End the Legal Loansharking Campaign, the *Mirror's* in-house investigations team, led by journalists Andrew

Penman and Nick Sommerlad, have consistently rallied against the ground made by payday lenders up and down the country. They were the journalists who signposted one particularly worrying company, Toothfairy Finance,[68] which still operates today. After reporting on the horror stories of high debts following extremely high interest loans, Penman and Sommerlad go on to talk about Bracknell and District Citizens Advice Bureau, which has accused Toothfairy of "harassing" one borrower "who had a debt relief order so should no longer have been chased for repayment". The Financial Ombudsman Service, they note, "is also probing complaints of harassment – one where Toothfairy allegedly took £1,140 when they were told to take £500 from a borrower's account."

The brain behind this operation is one Oliver Larholt. Larholt once spent 20 days in jail in 2002 after being convicted of possessing a flare pistol with intent to cause fear of violence.

On a post written up on the Credit Action Group forum,[69] one member recalls what it was like being a customer of Toothfairy. After taking out a loan of £100, failing to meet a payment and having requests of an extended payback period fall on deaf ears, the person reports that Toothfairy then decided to:

- [Call] my home number on a daily basis leaving information regarding who they are and my private account with them, that is that I have an outstanding loan and how much it was for, leaving the information open to third parties.

- [Send] me various emails each day telling me that they are adding fines to my loan.

- [Threaten] me with bailiffs and bankruptcy – for a £100 loan? I don't think so. They also said they would send bailiffs to all known addresses to collect goods up to nine times the value of the debt.

- [Tell] me they have passed my file to a solicitor and they are charging me £150 for this to be done. I have not heard from any solicitor or any debt collection agency (West Yorkshire Security Debt Collections) whom they say they have also consulted with.

Someone else in the comments thread recalled a similar story where nothing would be heard from the company for days and sometimes weeks, at which time charges have escalated to exorbitant levels.

I was told by one source that with loan book figures at around £2-3,000 daily, the company was extremely profitable. Unfortunately, too many similar stories are missed all the time. Online forums and social media help to foster an open culture whereby information can be shared quite easily between interested parties, but we still have a lot to thank the press for – and it is especially pleasing to find that the majority of press outlets in the UK are generally anxious about the growth of the payday loan industry.

Is Wonga a payday lender?

As the debate on payday lenders has become more frequent, one company stands out as being synonymous with UK payday lending itself: that company is Wonga.

In early November 2010 Stella Creasy MP tabled a 10-minute rule bill in Parliament, the Consumer Credit (Regulation and Advice) Bill, as well as organising an adjournment debate on November 9 discussing the bill with David Willetts, the minister for universities and science, as the principal government representative. Inside parliament, despite winning cross-party support for her bill, she struggled to move the still brand-new coalition government to do anything of worth. Soon after, the OFT decided it wasn't worth their while making good of her recommendation to cap the total cost of credit – saying that, overall, such lending markets worked 'reasonably well'.

Outside parliament she became known for her hard work campaigning on the subject in her constituency, giving the issue the sort of attention it hadn't received before. A war of words developed between Creasy and Wonga, the former focusing her attention on the company in comment pieces for the *Guardian* and on Twitter, while the latter returned fire in open letters. One of those letters from June 2011 raised the concern that Creasy's actions were turning into a "personalised campaign"; however, Wonga, on account of its size and presence, is the most obvious focus of such campaigns.

Wonga always seems to be happy to talk to the media; Errol Dameli, its chief executive, addresses public events and is perceived as both an entrepreneur and someone making the most of the creative technologies. Damelin, a recipient of the Credit Suisse Entrepreneur of the Year award in 2009, demands a level of respectability that would previously have been unheard of in moneylending circles. Wonga has built its presence through very widely circulated advertising campaigns. Anyone living in London in 2011 and 2012 will know that nearly every bus in the capital, and every tube carriage, has an advert by the company, all relating to how easy it is to take out loans from them, and how stressful banks are today (since replaced by bus adverts encouraging small businesses to take out Wonga loans).

One advert boasts that there are no hidden charges, while another goes with the tagline: 'Borrow what you need, not what suits your bank'. Another television advert has an animated family effectively explaining why APR is confusing and website controls make the process of borrowing more empowering for the lender (unlike other Wonga adverts in the past, this one will probably not be subject to report from the Advertising Standards Agency). This may not be the case for everyone, but since the advent of behavioural advertising, but every time I open my own hotmail email account, a link to Wonga's website appears.

Wonga is the biggest of several successful start-ups for Damelin. First there was Barzelan, a steel-wire company based in Israel and then Supply Chain Connect producing monitoring software in the US and UK – notable by how dissimilar these sectors are to finance. With an eye to challenging the slow processes that retail banks seem to embrace with consumer finance, Damelin with a team of two web developers started work on the Wonga algorithm, a largely secret set-up which assesses someone to evaluate what kind of borrower they will be. It works out if the person really is who they say they are and whether they are able to pay back the sum on the date they choose. Having accused banks of actually enjoying regulation and bureaucracy, Damelin was assured that since the internet is awash with personal details, from Facebook to the electoral register, that Wonga could make a reasonable character type with online tools – much to the cynicism of the retail bankers he met in Wonga's early days.

On the website, the potential borrower has to modify two horizontal sliders, with choices of up to £400 for a first-time user and £1,000 for seasoned customers that also shows how much will be paid back in total, as well as the legal obligation to show the APR – which is a representative 4,214 per cent at time of writing. It is claimed that around 30 pieces of simple information is found from the details a potential borrower taps in to the website, and Wonga is then able to find 6-8000 'data points' that relate to the individual. A decision can be made in around 15 minutes.

The company has benefitted from funding by Balderton Capital (£3.7 million in 2007); Accel Partners (which is also an investor in Facebook) added a further £14 million in 2009; £73 million came from Oak Investment Partners, Meritech Partners and the Wellcome Trust, which is not shabby at all for a company some have considered to be a legal loan shark.[70]

However, the company is not happy to be dubbed as this. It argues that it is not even a payday lender, because the borrower has to have a bank account, a job, is likely to be closer or above the median income range, and enjoy the option to pay back the loan, with interest, any time they want. Nobody is limited to the fixed date alone, unlike many other alternative lenders, because Wonga charges interest per day. In all other regards Wonga would prefer not to be perceived like the others. When I asked their communications director John Morwood to provide me with some details of the company, he sent me a survey completed by Populus. In their survey 56 per cent of customers used Wonga because 'it's faster', which as a percentage was down from 4 quarters previously where the figure was in the mid-70s. They had seen a recent increase in people who found it 'clear and trustworthy' and only very few said that it was 'my only option at the time'. 52 per cent said it was their first choice and only 3 per cent said it was their final choice.

I found some problems with the report. I was sent the information with an email from Mr Morwood asking me not to circulate it – I kept to my word on that. In fact, the information above is only information that Wonga's chief executive has made in public before (namely at the Centre for Responsible Credit's 2010 conference). Secondly, given that Wonga had lent out 1.5 million loans in total in the middle of 2011, at a time when their heavy advertising campaign was just getting started, the report could have benefitted from information such as sample size. In the customer satisfaction section of the report, there was 11 comments, all very nice, all strangely soundbite-esque, and completely without reference to who said them.

As my main contact, Mr. Morwood was extremely helpful. On asking about Wonga's business model, I happened to mention the sub-prime market, he said:

> "I want to make it clear this is absolutely not who Wonga's customers are. You must have a full bank account and debit

card to apply for starters. Our customers are very different to the home credit market, for example, and probably to the rest of the short-term, or payday sector too. That's not to suggest we never get it wrong, or you can't find poor examples, but we have provided more than 2.5 million loans since 2007 so this is not a niche service for a niche market."

Surprising then that in an interview published in March 2011 with the *Guardian* journalist Amelia Gentleman,[71] which gave Wonga the chance to showcase some examples of, in Gentleman's words, the 'web-savvy young professionals that the company believes it's catering to', instead representatives of the company plumped for a 53-year old lady called Susan, unemployed and dependent on disability benefits. Gentleman writes of Susan:

> "She finds that with the cost of living rising, her benefits sometimes don't stretch to the end of the month, and has taken out loans with Wonga to buy food, if she's caught short. She's a bit vague, but thinks she's taken out half a dozen loans with Wonga over the past few months ... She has had problems with credit cards before, and doesn't have an overdraft, but Wonga gave her credit very swiftly."

Not only will Susan's income be significantly less than that of the average person taking out a Wonga loan, according to Wonga themselves, she manages to be in that category of people who do not have access to mainstream forms of borrowing, has taken out nearly double the average payday loans per year per borrower (which is 3.5), has taken out exactly double the average amount of loans Wonga customers use, yet is still one of two examples Wonga felt was a good representative.

During the interview with Gentleman, Mr. Morwood said: "Sometimes we will make loans to people on significant benefits, but it is not something we do very frequently. It is very infrequent. I'm not going to say it doesn't happen."

Surprised, I contacted him straight away, asking how many times Susan had to apply for a loan before she got one from Wonga (bearing in mind that Wonga pride themselves on their sophisticated credit rating system, and also refuse two-thirds of all loan applications on the grounds that they are a responsible lender). He responded: "The customers we suggested [Amelia Gentleman] speak to were taken from a weekly feedback form where customers send us their thoughts of their own free will. There was no manipulating or hand-picking."

In other words, it was just chance that one of the positive feedback forms that week came from somebody who was radically different from the customer who Wonga believe they cater to predominantly. But it begs the question how many other similar chance encounters Wonga has? Rather than saying Susan is a successful example, I would suggest taking out loans with Wonga could be deleterious to her financial situation – particularly if it is often the case that she takes out these very high cost loans for food.

Though Wonga has been good enough to put itself in the limelight, it hasn't always received positive attention.

In January 2012 it was subject to what Alex Hern for the Left Foot Forward blog described as a 'spectacular Twitterstorm'[72] when Wonga tried to encourage students to take out a short-term loan with them to 'substitute part of their student loan'. Wonga claimed that, while their loans are much higher in interest rates than student loans, 'you only borrow it for a month and pay the loan back on a date that suits you'. As Hern points out in his blog post, nowhere in Wonga's advice is there any mention of the university hardship funds which offer low interest loans to students who are experiencing financial difficulties. Compass' Matthew Fulton pointed out from his own experience at the University of East Anglia, the short-term loans on offer for around £300 over a period of four months, until the student loan installment came in, for which the university charged 3 per cent interest. As he told me:

"They were financed by the student union and interest covered running costs alone."

The Helena Kennedy Foundation was one of the organisations that picked up the issue as soon as it hit Twitter. Wes Streeting is their chief executive and a former President for the National Union of Students. His opinion about Wonga targeting students is that:

> "Legal loan sharks like Wonga seeing students as a potential market is a symptom of the levels of hardship facing students in the current economic climate. Government student grants and loans barely cover living costs and working part time has become part and parcel of the modern student experience."

He went on to point out:

> "Wonga's suggestion that its short-term, high interest, loans are an alternative to low interest student loans provided by the government is highly misleading and self-serving. The government's student loans are probably the lowest interest loans that students will ever receive during their lives."

Under increasing pressure Wonga decided to take down its 'advice' that same day. There have been previous instances of the company responding to external pressure. After much pressure it was one of the first companies to acknowledge the problem of rollover loans, saying that ity had never benefitted from them. Making good on its word, in early 2012 it agreed to sign up to a new code of practice drawn up by the credit trade body the Finance & Leasing Association, restricting rollovers to three. Even Stella Creasy admitted in public, during an All Party Parliamentary Group (APPG) on Debt and Personal Finance, that Wonga was one of the few "compliant ones". Although, as another Labour MP, Yvonne Fovargue, told me:

> "If we had at our disposal a real-time tracking system, the government could concentrate more of its resources on tracing the illegal lenders – and besides, if the payday loan companies were doing what they say they are doing they should be happy with regulation".

Wonga has said before that it runs an ethical business. So, if this is to be believed, better regulation over the type of financial product it provides would not be detrimental for them. As most see it, state legislation is a solution ensuring responsible lenders are not competing in the same market as irresponsible ones, giving the industry a bad name. Indeed, this is one of the concerns that John Morwood expressed to me. In an email he wrote: "Wonga try to be as open as possible [for example with media and regulatory scrutiny – which I agree they do] but it is us who take the flack [while] the companies that don't engage carry on quietly."

This might be true, so the way in which to solve this problem is to regulate the industry better. I will deal with this issue at length in the next chapter.

CHAPTER 4
REGULATION – THE DISCUSSION
POINT

As DISCUSSED in the last chapter, press coverage of the payday lending industry is predominantly negative. One notable exception from this, is from journalist Alan O'Sullivan who, in an article for *This is Money*, wrote that of all payday lenders, Wonga may be the 'best bet.'[73] As this was a comparison with other payday lenders it might just be forgivable, but of course rarely is a payday loan anybody's best option. The question for most is, can Wonga's best bet be enough? Further still, can self-regulation for this industry be enough? Not just since Stella Creasy's high-profile campaign, but since the inception of the Consumer Credit Act 1974, governments have been asking what is the best way to regulate this industry. Does regulation need to be significantly redrawn now to protect the consumer from potentially predatory lenders in the payday loan market?

Regulation and monitoring bodies

The consumer credit regime in the UK, which includes payday loans, is currently regulated by the Consumer Credit Act 1974, and an amendment by the Consumer Credit Act 2006, with regulations which were enforceable in February 2011. The Act also dictates that unsecured loans should not exceed £25,000 and should run for a maximum of five years. At present, legislation is enforced by the Office of Fair Trading (OFT), which is able to withdraw credit licences where companies fail to comply with them or follow the OFT's Irresponsible Lending Guidance. Before 1974 the consumer credit industry was regulated by the 1948 Moneylenders Act, which capped interest rates at 48 per cent. Successor legislation abandoned the interest rate ceiling, which meant courts could decide on a case-by-case basis whether a credit agreement was either fair or exorbitant.

Throughout Labour's terms in the 2000s they took heed of growing outcries about consumer credit and the necessity of reform. Patricia Hewitt, then the Secretary for Trade & Industry, launched a report entitled 'Consumer Credit Market in the 21st Century' in December 2003 after much media uproar, before Gerry Sutcliffe, then MP for Bradford and Parliamentary Under-Secretary of State at the Department of Trade and Industry, with responsibility for employment as well as consumer and competition policy, outlined reforms to consumer credit market after reports of predatory lending and investigations by the Parliamentary Treasury Select Committee. As a KeyNote Market Intelligence report around the time (2005) noted:

> "The low entry costs in the UK consumer lending market, coupled with the increasing demand for personal loans attracted a host of new lenders".[74]

New laws to ensure responsible lending have for a long time been forthcoming, and the campaigns for them today are the result of many years of recommending further, better, legislation in parliament.

Payday loan companies are also independently monitored by the Finance & Leasing Association (FLA) which upholds a Lending Code for its payday loan company members. FLA members are required to complete an annual statement of compliance signed by the chief executive, and compliance visits are also undertaken. Stella Creasy MP accused the FLA in 2011 of only "tinkering around the edges". When I reminded Russell Hamblin-Boone, who is the head of communications at the Finance & Leasing Association, of Stella Creasy's comments, he replied:

> "The FLA Lending Code sets high standards of self-regulation for all parts of the consumer credit market. In February 2012, we launched a revised version to reflect regulatory and economic developments. This included the addition of a new section to cover short-term loans. We will review the Code regularly to ensure that it adapts and reflects changes across the credit market."

Codes and guidance

Indeed the FLA Lending Code does specify a limit to three rollover loans (which, as mentioned earlier, Wonga signed up to), which, if flouted, will see the forebearance measures in the Code activated, but the policies for payday companies seem rather tame, while the Code really isn't strong enough.

In SM Finlay's 2005 paper 'Predictive models of expenditure and over-indebtedness for assessing the affordability of new consumer credit applications'[75] he studies mainstream banks selling personal loans and credit cards, noting that while credit lenders were looking at a borrowers' income and credit history, many were not doing enough to evaluate outgoings as a factor in how affordable, and subsequently how responsible, a loan application was. Precisely the same problem, as can be seen above, is the case with payday lenders. In fact, evidence suggests that rollover loans are profitable for a lender, so rules looking at responsible lending in this way, while beneficial for the consumer, is less profitable for the lender.

In 2010 the OFT's guidance for creditors on irresponsible lending points out that:

"All assessments of affordability should involve a consideration of the potential for the credit commitment to adversely impact on the borrower's financial situation, taking account of information that the creditor is aware of at the time the credit is granted."

One of the elements that constitutes affordability by the OFT is "the borrower's existing and future financial commitments including any repayments due in respect of other financial products and significant non-credit commitments … for example, payments relating to rent, council tax, utility bills and hire etc." Also any reasonably foreseeable future changes in the level of the borrower's disposable income – for example, "if the borrower is close to retirement age and facing a significant fall in disposable income".

Lenders like Wonga assert that they only lend to a particular type of person, on a particular wage, who will make good on their loan and not require rollovers, but what the OFT says should be factored in responsible lending is, importantly, existing and future financial commitments.

Although good in writing, this was all very reliant on self-regulation and the OFT was still not for changing on caps on either interest or total cost of credit. The formal response by the Department for Business, Innovation and Skills and HM Treasury on consumer credit published in November 2011 held the same view. Where concerns have been raised they seek to improve the high cost credit market by introducing enhanced consumer protections in their codes of practice. However, they accept evidence that an interest cap on credit would do more harm than good, risking barriers to some consumers' ability to get mainstream credit, and they do not believe the case has been made for high cost credit sellers to have wealth warnings attached to their products. There is no evidence, they say, that it will deter consumers. In other words, more recommendations, but less willingness to intervene. When I asked Sarah Brooks of Consumer Focus about how to better regulate the payday lending industry, she said: "Self-regulation has not worked in this area. The code of practice that industry agreed was not robust enough to tackle the problems in the market and lacked effective mechanisms for monitoring and enforcement."

When I asked Stella Creasy how she viewed the current coalition government's work around consumer finance regulation and the payday lending industry specifically, she said she was happy that the issue is on the table at last, but found it frustrating that the government have issued a commission for Bristol University to do another very long piece of work on the matter. This relates to a long project that Ed Davey, when he was the Minister for Employment Relations, Consumer and Postal Affairs, asked the Personal Finance Research Centre (PFRC) to carry out. Creasy is clearly frustrated that while consumers, including her own constituents, are being ripped off right now, the government, which is not acting nearly fast enough to solve a clear and present problem, is wasting more time on a long, possibly fruitless project. Furthermore, she is acutely aware that the PFRC has previously come out against price caps, and may give similar results.

One encouraging point is the creation of the Financial Conduct Authority (FCA). Going live at the end of 2012, the FCA is the successor regulatory body to the Financial Services Authority (FSA) which will assume responsibility for protecting consumers and market regulation. Its early promises, set out in a government White Paper, are to intervene early where potential risks may occur and be tougher and bolder on consumer concerns using new powers of intervention and enforcement. Trust in the financial sector, as FSA chief executive Hector Sands said on the release of the FCA's approach document, is at an "all time low". It is the task of the FCA to find "the right balance between the benefits of early intervention and the consequent risks of reducing choice and raising costs". In other words, it will be raising appropriate questions about how much the government should do, while providing clarity on the question of responsibilities on the part of consumers and industry alike.

At the APPG on Personal Debt and Finance in February 2012, David Fisher, director of consumer credit at the OFT (which the FCA will eventually replace in responsibility of consumer credit regulation), said that he hoped the FCA would bring the prospect of greater regulation, as at present there is "a very light-touch regime". He implies that this is because the OFT runs on only £11 million with 120 staff in the consumer credit office – the implication being that it is too cash and resource strapped to do much when receiving complaints.

He goes on:

> "It can take the OFT a long time to get businesses out of the market. The OFT can go up to and include stopping consumer credit licences; however, [and with consideration of the financial and operational difficulties mentioned above] it could take many months when they appeal on the first-tier tribunal, then further time when there is the second-tier tribunal on law … could take a few years."

All this before we even mention how concerned the OFT are about new technological products.

On the same panel was John Lamidey of the CFA, who stated that: "Whatever you believe, regulation was the problem [and the] Cheque Act of 1992 had as an unintended consequence cheque fraud, which brought about cheque cashers … and by 1994 cheque cashers had their own trading association and the payday lending industry was born out of this."

It is of course no surprise that someone whose clients are payday lenders is against the regulation of that industry, but nobody I have spoken to on this subject is unaware of the unintended consequences of 'squeezing supply but doing nothing about demand'. Any regulation must look at its wider implications, and even the most hardened enemy of the payday lending industry knows this. The flipside to this is that if you simply let payday lenders self-regulate, it's not the ones that can be trusted that you need to worry about. It is the ones that do not play by the rules, and regulatory authorities, by upping their game on the industry, are fast finding this out. For example, in March 2012, the OFT revoked the licence of payday lender, Yes Loans, after it was reported as having lost patience with their "deceitful and oppressive business practices", noting that it "encouraged customers to take out expensive short-term loans – rather than products they had initially asked about – and misled them into believing it was a loan provider rather than a credit broker." The difference being that the former issues loans whereas the latter seeks out the right loan for the individual. The odds of less regulation are not stacked in the industry's favour. But for many, that regulation won't be enough; it will only provide olive-sized improvement.

At the time of writing, it is difficult to put on the news or listen to the radio without another item about PPI redress and compensation payments. The mis-selling of financial products only begs for more power for bodies such as the FCA. According to the approach document, the government along with the FCA will have the power for product intervention and to direct firms to withdraw or amend misleading financial products. Owing to recent interest by the press and in parliament, payday lenders will be under the radar. But the antipathy which the regulatory authorities express over the topic of interest rate caps, or even caps on the total cost of credit, is far from accepted.

Arguments for and against price controls on credit

The arguments for and against have always been compelling. Unlike in Germany and France, the UK has no price controls for credit – it allows the market to run itself. As Veronika Thiel in 'Doorstep Robbery' anticipates: "The government will say the poor in Germany and France are worse off. This ignores the facts. In those countries the poor have wider access to credit and there are fewer adults without bank accounts."

Thiel continues:

> "From data on consumer credit market volumes, it becomes immediately clear that supply of credit in Germany and France is not as abundant as in the UK [and yet, there is] little by way of evidence for illegal lending in France and Germany (from Institut für Finanzdienstleistungen [Institute for Financial Services] and during email correspondence with the Fédération des Caisse d'Epargne [French Savings Banks Association])."

Policis claims to have evidence to the contrary. "In the wake of a recent sharp reduction in the rate ceiling in Japan", it says, "consumer loan applications have fallen by close to two thirds in two years, accompanied by growth of illegal lending usually facilitated by organised criminals, and bankruptcies have risen."

For Policis, ceilings only cause credit exclusion; more will turn to revolving credit and gain adverse credit ratings, creating harmonious conditions for unlicensed lenders, for which more competition is the only realistic antidote.

In their 2008 report on the impact of interest rate ceilings in Australia,[76] Policis, benchmarking against other European countries, the UK included, found that cash advances on credit cards would move low income Australians from high cost credit to revolving credit, which would have a negative impact upon their credit ratings, causing, among other things, an increased risk of default and credit exclusion. Rate ceilings would mean lenders restructure pricing to accommodate for constraints and would thus be ineffectual in reducing cost burden to the borrower, and overall could add price on to the total cost of credit as the payday lending industry shrinks.

I asked Gerard Brody, the director of policy and campaigns at Consumer Action in Australia, what changes had been made to the regulatory system, to which he replied new federal legislation was enacted at this time, attempting to harmonise state and territory legislation on consumer credit, under the National Consumer Credit Protection Act 2009. It ought to be noted that the Australian government does not impose interest rate restrictions, but allows this responsibility to be devolved to individual states and territories. Introduced under the Act was a national licensing framework for all consumer credit providers, and obligations included being members of an external dispute resolution scheme such as a financial or credit ombudsman. I asked Mr Brody whether there had there been a significant decrease in lower income households getting credit, owing to the four states or territories of Australia that have a 48 per cent cap on APR on loans. He replied: "We are not aware that there has been a reduction of lower income households obtaining credit and neither are we aware of any rise in illegal loan sharks."

There are a couple of reasons for this, including avoidance mechanisms such as sham brokerage fee arrangements, cross-border lending, and requirements to purchase 'financial literacy DVDs', which are clearly ways around making up for lost earnings (which, to be fair, Policis rightly anticipated). Mr Brody went on to say: "Access to affordable credit to those that can pay back small amount loans is improving with government investment in community lending like the No Interest Loans Scheme, and Step Up [not-for-profit loan developed by the National Australia Bank and Good Shepherd Youth & Family Service of between $800 and $3000 for low incomes families at a basic interest rate of 3.99 per cent pa], supported by National Australia Bank." Mr Brody was honest about what his organisation would like to see done about the payday lending industry in Australia – with a tone that would be rare in the UK: "Most payday lending is advanced to people to pay for day-to-day expenses such as food and rent, and a responsible lender would not advance such loans. Access to this type of irresponsible credit is not a positive thing, and can serve to exacerbate a borrower's financial situation."

Policis was trying to highlight the unintended consequences in their report, but clearly with avoidance mechanisms and investment in community lending, it hasn't escaped attention in Australia. That Australia has seen a ballooning of payday loans from the years 2002-3 to 2008-9, Consumer Action has decided, according to Mr Brody, "There is no need for the payday loan industry and it does not serve a public interest purpose." He continued, "While some people might need access to short-term financial relief, this should be provided by government income support; support from service providers in terms of allowing to pay bills by affordable installment; and further growth of affordable no interest and low-interest loans." And on this point, to return to something Veronika Thiel says in her report, "Interest rate caps have to be levelled among a series of other regulations and interventions."

In 2010 Profesor Dr. Udo Reifner, Sebastien Clerc-Renaud, and RA Michael Knobloch from the Institut für Finanzdienstleistungen e.V., in association with the Zentrum für Europäische Wirtschaftsforschung GmbH, submitted to the European Commission a comprehensive inventory of the types of interest rates that exist in EU member states. What was found was that countries with a relative interest rate ceiling, based on either market rate or money market rate, as opposed to an absolute ceiling rate (operated in Greece, Ireland and Malta without impact to the economy), have proved to be effective in countries like Belgium, Estonia, France, Germany, Italy, the Netherlands, Poland, Portugal, Slovakia, Spain, and Slovenia. The results coincide with the assumption that strict interest rate ceilings are the most effective – a result which should be most apposite in the UK where, it is reported by the professors, "Payday loans are most important ... along with the Netherlands and Latvia."

The social fund and crisis loans

The low interest support loans that Mr. Brody spoke about in Australia are not, as most will know or assume, alien to the UK.

Norman Fowler, who served as a member of Margaret Thatcher's cabinet from 1981 to 1990, instituted what came to be known as the 'Fowler reforms' of the social security system, under which the social fund was introduced. It was set up in the knowledge that for low income families, financial shocks and emergency expenses are very difficult to account for, particularly for those with little or no savings. The fund could be sought from government to cover funeral costs, the costs of a new baby, and one-off payments for large items such as furniture, and was levelled out alongside community care grants and crisis loans. It also covered winter fuel payments for female pensioners.

Many over the years have said the social fund needed reform-ing, but what the coalition government has decided to do is remove central government responsibility over it. According to the Department of Work and Pension's 'Equality impact assessment for the new local welfare assistance to replace Social Fund Community Care Grants and Crisis Loans for general living expenses', in 2009/10 alone over 263,000 non-repayable Community Care Grants (which can be claimed through the social fund) were awarded at a cost of £141 million, with the average initial award being £437. On top of this in 2009/10, around 2.7 million Crisis Loans were awarded to help people deal with emergencies, at a cost of £233 million. The average award was £82. Applicants may be awarded a Crisis Loan for four specific reasons:

- Items or services;
- Rent in advance;

- General living expenses;

- Alignment payments to fill in until first benefit payment.

These are being replaced by local provision delivered by local authorities. But the social fund is being binned.

When I interviewed Helen Goodman MP, she told me of its vital importance; however, she said:

> "It needed to be tweaked, sure – for many on benefits it was adequate for outgoings but not fit for if your fridge broke. Also claimants didn't get a written statement so they didn't know how much was going out in repayment. But instead the coalition government has got rid of it."

The need for a 'tweaking' was obvious. As Paul Jones noticed, the social fund could be deducted out of income support or Job Seekers' Allowance. The maximum loan was £206 over a period of 78 weeks, interest-free. However, repayments were not flexible as with other loans. Many reported to Jones that they received less than they had asked for and the method of deductions did not account for week-on-week financial trouble. Policis research showed that some had used high cost credit as an alternative to interest-free social fund loans, either because they had been turned away or had received less than they had hoped from the loan.

Polly Toynbee in her book 'Hard Work' noted that a recipient could be waiting weeks for their loan to come through, and the amount received considerably less than expected. To make matters worse for the very vulnerable, social fund rules say that people cannot get hold of their loan until they have the keys to their new place of residence if, for example, they have just come from a hostel. This means that they could be in their flat for weeks before being able to buy anything. Alternatives would run thin at this stage.

Reading through the DWP report, I see no rationale for reform that suggests a localised system will be any better, just that it should benefit the most vulnerable because it is local. It doesn't mention how it can be better delivered, perhaps through credit unions (as Jane Perry pointed out in her 2010 'Paying over the odds'[77]), or how complaints like those on benefits and repayment flexibility can be addressed. There is nothing on long-term needs which will impact upon the financial education of the frequent user – unlike in Labour's plans for social fund reform. This government, whether intentionally or not, is creating more barriers by scrapping the social fund and it should seriously reconsider.

Recommendations

Before witnessing Stella Creasy debate her 10-minute bill in Parliament, (which I later reported for the *Guardian*'s Comment is Free section[78]) one of the things I expected was for there to be a clear divide between those for whom regulation was the only realistic approach to curb predatory lending to the vulnerable, and those with faith in the market. I was pleasantly surprised to learn that even some of Parliament's free market advocates were not so idealistic as to suppose there was some invisible hand benevolently drifting over the heads of this industry waiting to intervene, invisibly, so as not to trouble politicians.

One MP I was very excited to meet was Damian Hinds, the Conservative MP for East Hampshire. He told me that 10 years ago, when, as a free-market economics advocate, he took an interest in debt issues, he was adamant that market rules applied, that predatory lenders would be priced out by more competition in the market, which sought to undercut the Fabian-esque instinct towards more nanny-state and more government regulation. But now his mind has been changed. "Normal market rules do not apply here", he says without a flinch, "but beware of easy solutions to problems". He means the argument for capping interest rates. He points out that if you cap APR at, say, 15 per cent then two things are certain: "that short-term lending disappears and you restrict the legal services to high-risk customers". Another reason Hinds would not want to price out some types of high interest lending with a cap without anything to replace it is because it does serve some important functions, but not in the way one might assume.

As an economist he naturally wants to look at things through the prism of the rational consumer, in which case the question arises as to why would someone pay over the odds on a loan when there are other things available (assuming, of course, that the consumer is aware of all options and is making a value judgment on what product is best for them – not always the case, especially in this market as Hinds is well aware). Hinds says: "The reason can often be because people sometimes tend towards higher interest for familiarity. Word-of-mouth possibly?" It is for this reason that alternatives should be sought to high cost credit, while keeping those elements that obviously appeal to people, like familiarity, that often see rational consumers make seemingly irrational choices. The not-for-profit home credit market, researched by the Joseph Rowntree Foundation, is one example.

Not all free market advocates share Hinds' approach. Dr Richard Wellings, the deputy editorial director for the Institute of Economic Affairs, told me: "If companies aren't allowed to charge a risk premium that reflects the high chance of default then they will withdraw from the market, forcing customers to use so-called loan sharks."

This answer would only be sufficient if the regulation on the table today ensured prices reflect a break-even point for lenders – which *may* force some companies to close shop. In fact, both an interest rate cap and a cap on the total cost of credit would likely take into consideration the risk profile of a customer. But where Dr Wellings' answer fails is on the point of regulation; given his response it would seem that the only reason to regulate an industry was to stop it making money –

which is, unfortunately, a typical response extended towards regulation. Usual market rules do not apply here, and good regulation is needed in this market to curb predatory and irresponsible lending, such that would have serious effects on vulnerable families.

It was clear from Dr Wellings' next response that he was never likely to understand this anyway, saying: "If they [payday loan customers] were prudent people they wouldn't need such a loan in the first place." An answer that I find ill-informed and infuriating.

Many agree that interventionist approaches ought to be taken, but of what kind?

The OFT's report into high cost credit in 2010 said that the rollover cap should be on five loans, something which Consumer Focus also recommended in the same year. Consumer Focus' Director of Financial Services Sarah Brooks also said that on top of a rollover cap, her organisation has "called for better affordability checks including credit checks. We are also concerned about marketing and use of continuous payment authorities to collect debts." Other frequently cited interventions are total cost caps. Tax economist Richard Murphy back in 2003[79] suggested that: "Caps should not just be on interest, but on total charges so companies do not add those charges where they will lose elsewhere."

Murphy points out three elements where charges stem from: interest; arrangement fees for setting up the loan; and collection fees, all of which risk price increases if only one element is capped.

While payday lenders like to try to present themselves as a helping hand, they are actually a detriment to people in vulnerable financial positions, and there seems to be little by way of evidence that they will put the brakes on this themselves through self-regulation. Stella Creasy told me that in a perfect world she would like to see an industry and consumer regulatory model that is fit for purpose, overseeing and evaluating what counts as responsible lending, as well as a cap on the total cost of credit which the industry should be involved in when deciding.

Elsewhere in the Labour camp, it is the opinion of Derek Twigg MP that payday lenders, when they breach the rules of responsibility as OFT recently found, should be treated, not as though they were committing consumer crimes, but theft. Ian Murray MP confirmed his commitment to a cooling-off period for people spiralling into debt. Yvonne Forague MP said that if we had at our disposal a real-time tracking system, the government could concentrate more of its resources on tracing the illegal lenders. More specifically still, Nic Daikin MP, also one of the signatories of the End the Legal Loansharking campaign, pointed out that Britain should be using the system employed in Florida. "With the Veritac system, the state [in Florida] has a real-time database on people who are taking loans – this provides a single source of judging how many loans a person is taking out at one time, and responsibility lies with the state, as well as with the lender and the borrower themselves."

The think tank Compass in their Mini Toolkit on legal loan sharks give a step-by-step guide on setting up grassroots campaigns against payday loan shops. A campaign in Norwich culminated in a local branch of The Money Shop agreeing to meet a local End the Legal Loansharking team, advertise free debt advice in shop and actively support local credit unions.

But demands on payday lenders will not be enough. It is still problems within the banking sector that allows payday lending to thrive. As Consumer Focus pointed out in their report 'Keeping the plates spinning', with banking sector reform should come clear fee structures, an emergency borrowing facility, and fair bank charges for being overdrawn. One of Veronika Thiel's recommendations is for the creation of a community reinvestment act which will promote transparency in all lenders, and where banks that do not lend sufficiently in local communities are forced to sponsor a local affordable lender. Doorstep lenders, she points out, should also be compelled to make people aware of cheaper alternatives. Another issue is on credit scoring – the criteria on which a loan can be assessed for risk. Thiel highlights that a lack of credit history can be interpreted as a bad credit rating, and the outcome could be difficulty in applying for personal loans, even though the individual has been, in Veronika's words, financially prudent.

Finally, research needs to be funded, perhaps from the government, studying the possible links between growth in payday lenders and insolvency rates. Studies in the US have pointed out that payday loans, though not directly the cause of it, can bolster chances of the need for personal insolvency, but, obviously, as it is US-specific, cannot be applicable here. Indeed, looking at other instances where advice is sought after a payday loan has gone wrong, one can see how the logic adds up. David Rodger from the Debt Advice Foundation told me: "People will come on to us and give us a whole raft of other information before saying 'then I took out a payday loan'. When people get into serious debt because of them [payday loans], they see themselves as a failure."

Debt management practices need to change also. Paul Crayston of the Money Advice Trust said:

> "The reality is that the high cost of bankruptcy is preventing many people from going insolvent even though it would be the best option for them [this can be people with debts over £15,000, with little or no surplus income]. The underlying economic problem therefore isn't reflected in the insolvency figures, which aren't accounting for those who would go bankrupt if they could afford the fees. That cheaper forms of insolvency – individual voluntary agreements (IVAs) and debt relief orders (DROs) – are rising corroborates this theory."

At the start of February 2012 the Guardian reported that the UK had seen a "three-year low on personal insolvencies"[80]. But an extra look shows that while the fall in insolvency figures was accounted for mostly by the drop in bankruptcies, cheaper options such as IVAs and had both risen. Not everything is fine in the personal finance department after all.

Matthew Whitaker for the Resolution Foundation pointed out in 2010 that the incomes of the bottom three-fifths of the UK population failed to keep up with rising prosperity, seeing their share of national income fall from 40 to 33 per cent between 1977 and 2008.[81] So why were we all kept quietly happy during the so-called boom period of 1997 and 2007? As researchers at the PFRC put it, that 'boom' was sustained by "the dramatic growth in the mainstream consumer credit market". They go on to note that "the UK's 'technical recession' has ended ... the 'practical recession' is in full swing with households feeling the effects of the economic crisis more sharply than they were two years ago."[82]

There are winners and losers here. The losers, unsurprisingly, are those who have seen their living standards shrink, or have maybe never seen their living standards rise. The winners? The winners, of course, are the payday lenders, which even in the bad times will see their product surge, and which prey on those who are most insecure – for which we have ineffectual and ill-considered economic and financial policies largely to blame.

CHAPTER 5
A NOTE ON ILLEGAL LOANSHARKING

A CONCERN since the recession is that illegal loansharking will increase. As with many underground crimes, where the victim is often reluctant to report, it is hard to tell precisely what's occurring. In an early 2012 report by the BBC, it was pointed out that "300,000 families [were] in hock to loan sharks in England alone – and they are just the ones who have come forward."[83] This is an incredible rate of growth compared to the 2009 figure of 165,000 given by the PFRC and Policis.

Your friendly local loan shark

At the 2010 Centre for Responsible Debt Convention, Tony Denny, the Financial Inclusion Partnership Officer, reported back on the work of the seven illegal moneylending teams. His statistics found that 65 per cent of loan shark users found them through a friend, 44 per cent knew the loan shark before borrowing money from them and 66 per cent had other debts (that averaged around £7,000). Another very concerning figure Denny gave was that 43% considered their loan shark a friend.

But this should not surprise us too much. A loan shark will do good business if he or she acts like a friend, not to mention cases where it is incumbent upon a debt collector, often not the loan shark themselves, to pretend friendship with a debtor. It is often forgotten that the collectors are sometimes just as vulnerable as the people they are collecting from. Research by Karen Rowlingson and Elaine Kempson for the Policy Studies Institute in 1994[84] found that, out of the eight collectors they had personally interviewed, three had been physically attacked, two of them by dogs.

It is also forgotten that loan sharks themselves, though their business is not justified in any way, can be on the receiving end of hardship. One of the counterintuitive stories about loan sharks can be found in Paul Jones' 2001 report 'Access to Credit'.[85] He points out that money lenders were not always the hard men that might have first been imagined. Often the job was being carried out by local women, recognisable in their communities. Jones spoke to an unsuccessful loan shark who was in a car crash, received a few thousand pounds and was unsure as to what to do with it. She took the decision to lend to her friends, charging £20 interest on a £100 loan for three months. This slightly odd entrepreneurial attempt was losing her money hand over fist, particularly on petrol money while collecting. Her 'friends' would eventually just not open the door to her or fail to return her calls.

This doesn't excuse such behaviour, but in order to understand loansharking properly it is worth considering. It has a historical precedent. Some loansharking appeared as normal in the 1870s through to the 1900s in American cities, for example. There were no bouts of violence during debt collections for example, and missed payments were levelled with a threat that the lender would tell the debtors' employer, which though it is very serious, doesn't compare to the stories we hear on the news today regarding loan sharks. The worst that could happen, often, was that a debtor would be frowned upon since 'respectable opinion' considered consumer borrowing a sign of moral weakness.

This type of loansharking was not to last forever. In January 1935, an incident took place where a 23 year-old clerk was beaten outside his place of employment for failing to meet the costs of a $6 interest on a loan of $10 – this signposted an important change in illegal money lending. The special investigator overlooking the incident, Thomas E. Dewey, a man not afraid of trying to take down mafia thugs, and who stood twice as the Republican candidate for President in 1944 and 1948, arrested 27 individuals for loansharking activities in October of that same year. Not only did the game start to change, but enthusiasm by enforcement agencies increased, too.

There were enormous degrees of difference between the salary lenders of the late 1800s and early 1900s and the racketeer loan sharks, particularly in the manner with which they handled repayments. The similarities were in charging illegal rates of interest. Of course, in America there has been a history of usury laws and in many states interest has for a long time been capped. This isn't, admittedly, a purely positive thing. Interest rate caps in New York and Chicago were once so low (around 6 per cent) that virtually every credit lender had to operate illegally in order to operate at all.

The key thing to remember is not the degrees of difference in unlicensed lenders, from the ones who are themselves vulnerable to the ones who smash windows to get their money back, but that it is all illegal, and the need for it implies desperation that should be addressed. According to the Index of Multiple Deprivation from the UK Department for Communities and Local Government: "Loan sharking occurs mostly in deprived micro-communities, particularly amongst the 1.4 million that both fall into the poorest quintile of households and the most deprived areas."

Fighting the criminals

Stories from local communities themselves back up the feeling that loan sharks, by and large, are exploitative and prey on the vulnerable. A news item carried by the North West Evening Mail focused its attention on the Four Groves estate in Barrow,[86] where community stalwart Pauline Charnely pointed out that illegal loan sharks were targeting areas where many were "struggling to survive on benefits, some with small children to care for, others with drug or alcohol problems." Another example is 69-year-old Kanadasaba Nadarajah,[87] a loan shark who preyed upon poorer communities in Sri Lankan neighbourhoods in East Ham, London. After being caught, Nadarajah had the choice of paying back £370,257.68 to the courts or facing up to three and a half years in prison. One particular ledger book detailed almost 800 loans, indicating that approximately £1.3million worth of loans had been given out illegally over eight years.

One judge, Honour Judge Lever, who was present during the conviction of one loan shark, Michael Morris, a former British super-featherweight champion who operated from Armstrong's Boxing Gym in Salford, described Morris' crimes – 800 loan agreements through his illegal business M.A.M. Finance – as "murder of the soul".[88] This is a very reasonable summation of loan sharks' actions, and for committing these crimes the punishment should fit. Morris was ordered to pay back the £260,000 he made in assets and served three years in prison.

Some criminals, however, will never be sufficiently punished for the crimes they committed. I spoke to Carol Highton, founder of the Brian Shields Trust, which she bravely established after her son had taken his own life after receiving years of intimidation from a loan shark. "After losing my son I found that I just kept hitting a brick wall with the police – they just didn't seem interested in what I was telling them about the illegal money lender Paul Nicholson." She recalled her son telling her about a 'friend' who had got himself in trouble with a loan shark. It was only with hindsight that Carol realised that the 'friend' was in fact Brian himself. "One of the reasons I set up the trust", she continued, "was that I was so angry that nobody was listening to what I was telling them about this horrendous man and his henchmen." Nicholson was able to terrorise other individuals and families for two years, during which time "he went on to even rape one of his victims as well as prostituting others, blackmailing and intimidating hundreds of people into giving into his horrendous demands."

Brian became involved with Nicholson through his workplace. Carol said: "His boss was an associate of Nicholson's and he befriended Brian and his workmates. He got to know personal things about my son and the family and then used this information against Brian which then made him very vulnerable because he then had this extra pressure to protect the family." On asking Carol what she felt was the appropriate punishment for a loan shark, she told me "This would depend on the severity of the criminal activities of the illegal lender, for example Paul Nicholson was a vicious bully who over a span of four years intimidated, beat up, raped, prostituted and blackmailed his victims into paying extortionate rates. He quite rightly deserved his indefinite life sentence."

But seeking punishment on loan sharks is not the sum total of her work by any stretch. She wants to see awareness raised around the issue and more scrutiny on who receives money lending licences. Extremely worryingly, Carol told me, was that "Paul Nicholson was issued a [money lending] licence in 2004 even though he had a criminal record for very serious offences involving drugs and weapons." It's a familiar story, one that should give the regulators a headache.

But this isn't to do down the work that is being put in today to try and curb illegal moneylending. Indeed, Carol praises the work of the Illegal Moneylending teams, who she and the Brian Shields Trust have worked with in order to keep the streets safe and avoid episodes like the one Carol herself faced. Funded by the Department of Business Innovation and Skills, the Illegal Moneylending team was set up as a pilot in Birmingham in 2004 to cover the West Midlands, with a sister scheme piloted in Scotland. It was a huge success and received further government funding from both BIS and the Financial Inclusion Fund, allowing for an expansion in numbers. By the end of 2010 the team covered the North West, South East, East of England and Yorkshire and Humberside, alongside six smaller teams. The teams are now divided up by England, Scotland and Wales.

They of course work according to the Consumer Credit Act 1974, the Proceeds of Crime Act 2002 and the Theft Act 1968 (which covers the demanding of money with menaces/blackmail). As the Policis evaluation of the teams pointed out,[89] the law against illegal money lending is now being proactively enforced, with 280 illegal lenders arrested and 163 proceedings instituted against 185 defendants. Further, "The project in 2006 had relieved (where the payment burden to the lender is lifted) 14,000 victims – four out of five victims where the money lender they approached has been arrested [and] POCA (Proceeds of Crime Act) gains were in the region of £9.1m, which would accrue to society as a whole, while the overall total net benefit generated by the IML project is estimated at £28.3m."

The barriers to the teams' good work remains how much they can do when the victims are, as previously mentioned, reluctant to speak out. Sarah-Jane Lynch, the Communications Officer of the England Illegal Money Lending Team told me, on the subject of shame, "It is very difficult to get people to speak out but we run a 24/7 hotline for people to report loan sharks to us in confidence – anonymously if they wish. People can also report via email text or Facebook." In order to overcome such barriers, Lynch says that the team itself has "a 17 strong team of LIAISE officers (leads in awareness intelligence support and education) who engage with communities and get the message about avoiding and reporting loan sharks out there. They organise a variety of awareness raising events initiatives and campaigns to involve the public and provide information and advice." She continued that: "Once a loan shark is reported to us a full investigation will be carried out into the scale of the money lending and they will be prosecuted through the courts. We've had just over 200 prosecutions so far, leading to 128 years of custodial sentences and supported over 18,000 victims."

As for the horror stories, Lynch recounts that:

> "In terms of APR the highest we've seen was calculated as equivalent to 131,000 per cent. In terms of monetary value one guy borrowed £250 and paid back £90,000 over two decades. In the most extreme cases we have seen loan sharks resort to violence including one case where the loan shark raped the victim and another where the victim was kidnapped and attacked with a machete but these are rare, and in the most part the intimidation is enough for them to keep victims repaying without resorting to this."

One of the things the teams do, as part of their work to counsel victims when a loan shark has been caught, is to get them to join a local credit union and take measures to organise their finances better. When I asked about the relationship dynamic between credit unions and illegal moneylending teams, Sally Chicken, the volunteer director of Ipswich and Suffolk Credit Union, said:

> "They have involved us several times at the earliest possible stages ... we went into a workplace with Trading Standards to tell staff about the credit union when the team had arrested a workplace loan shark. When the teams are invited to speak to organisations, they always take our information, and have suggested that we go and visit too. They will ask us to leaflet an area, and have offered us money from the proceeds of crime which has paid for leaflets, and also bonus offers to help get savers. Our current offer is: 'Refer a friend and get £10, the friend also gets £10 and the joining fee is waived.'"

In the context of payday lenders, one obvious and important thing that differentiates them from illegal lenders is regulation. Payday lenders are constantly on a mission to appear respectable, often raising illegal loan sharks to benchmark against. But just because the horror stories attached to illegal lenders are just that – horrific - this should not in any way detract against the harm caused by them and their high street operations.

I should like to note that a comparison in behaviour between payday lenders and illegal loan sharks is, more often than not, very weak – we would miss the point of why opposition to payday lending is needed if we dignify this comparison any more. But certainly one argument sticks – namely that if the government were to do more about properly regulating the payday lending industry, and making sure individuals, like Paul Nicholson, are unable to successfully apply for credit licenses, then it could spend more time concentrating on the illegal variant of moneylending. Indeed the 2010 study on interest rate restrictions in the EU found that there is no convincing comprehensive data to evaluate the hypothesis that interest rate restrictions lead to a substantial illegal market in lending. While this should remind us of the need for such a comprehensive study in the UK, currently lacking, it ought to highlight that the government are on the wrong side of the argument when they suggest that more restrictions on the payday lending industry leads necessarily to vulnerable people seeking loans on the black market.

CHAPTER 6
THE FUTURE OF LENDING – CREDIT SELLING IN AN AGE OF HEIGHTENED CONSCIOUSNESS

MOST CAN AGREE, particularly after the John Vickers' Independent Commission on Banking, that business as usual is not an option. For many this implies that banking has to change. Payday lenders have achieved an unexpected level of perceived moral high ground by citing the banks' inability to lend as one reason why their product is both necessary and successful. This may be true, but by no means should imply the worth of the payday loan product. What should happen is that the banking sector should brace itself for real reform.

The need for financial reform

But, then, how long have commentators been saying this?

The recession perhaps has reminded us of the need for financial reform, but without the political will we might consider the fight lost. Back in 2010, still suffering the initial wounds of the global financial recession, Compass released a research paper entitled 'Banks We Can Believe In',[90] which offered some conclusions on how to get out of the current mess, and stay out of it. Its key solution was to iron out the basic contradiction of the banking model, namely to please both shareholders and be a vital part of a harmonious society. As the report points out, the crisis wasn't due to a few cowboys, but was systemic.

Part of what was hoped from Prime Minister David Cameron's speak on big society was the greater role for an expanded third sector and a renewed social banking sector. The thinking here being that with a more localised banking system, there would be less disparity between stakeholders and those using the banks themselves. During the Good Banking summit of 2010, it was reminded during a conversation on the 'postbank' that "Despite pledges from banks to increase lending to small businesses, the total amount being lent was 2 per cent down on 2010 in the first quarter of 2011 and in the two months to March." The Federation of Small Businesses reported that around 40 per cent of small businesses applying for credit were turned down by their bank. Of course, a real part of the problem is that banks are being encouraged to sit on capital rather than lend money out.

Two options seem to emerge (though there are more): we aim to reform the banks and build up viable alternative products through credit unions, or we forget the lot and try to realise a financial system entirely devoid of banks. In this section I discuss both.

Credit unions and other alternatives

Credit cooperatives were first introduced in Germany during the 1850s, according to Timothy Guinnane in his paper 'Cooperatives as Information Machines: German Rural Credit Cooperatives, 1883-1914'.[91] Smallholders and the landless relied heavily on informal lenders to pay down their debts, and only several German states had allowed the creation of specialist banks known as Sparkassen, or savings banks – so widely rolled-out cooperatives were a welcome intervention. By 1861 there were 364 Schulze-Delitzsch (as in Hermann Schulze-Delitzsch who founded several cooperatives in the 1840s and 1850s) credit cooperatives with nearly 49,000 members.

The first credit union in the UK was likely to have been born out of the first properly documented cooperative institution which was in Rochdale in 1844. As Ann-Marie Ward and Donal McKillop in their paper on the relationship between credit union objects and cooperative philosophies[92] point out, though Rochdale probably wasn't the first cooperative institution, it certainly was the most successful of the day, especially in terms of its reach, and is recognised as the first modern cooperative on which many others were subsequently modelled. Paul Jones in his 2007 paper on credit unions[93] noted that political support for the institutions didn't occur until the 1980s/1990s as they started to become "part of local and central government discourse on tackling poverty and disadvantage." Soon into the mid-1990s it was realised that the operations model for credit unions had to change from one focusing only on the most disadvantaged, to something more encompassing of wider society. From 1999, so says Jones, the Association of British Credit Unions (ABCUL), the sector's largest trade association, decided to encourage credit unions to operate a little more like a business. There was 'robust business planning', the introduction of IT operations employed staff rather than just volunteers.

Another part of the new model of credit unions, which was prompted by ABCUL's attempt to emulate the best from international credit unions, was what Jones calls the "maximisation of savings". The move away from credit unions being unfairly dubbed the 'poor persons' bank', and appealing to more middle class clients, meant that more money was being saved, and this gave credit unions the opportunity to lend money out at low interest. This both tied in with the anti-poverty credit unions' commitment to steering low-income families away from high interest sub-prime lenders, as well as helping the local economy as borrowers tended to spend their income locally. But what held many credit unions back was funding. Under Blair's Labour there was a commitment towards more funding for credit unions, which was perfectly consistent with the 'third way' appeal to a savings culture to assist with welfare, such as the Savings Gateway and the Child Trust Fund.

There is still discord between the boots on the ground opinion of credit unions and ABCUL. I asked Sally Chicken how credit unions could make themselves more appealing than short-term lenders online or on the high street, to which she replied that her union was already making short-term loans.

> "We are already very appealing to people once they have heard of us, so we really just need a good loud marketing campaign, I don't understand why ABCUL is so against a national marketing awareness campaign ... in the US there are still such public information radio ads, even though there is already high awareness. We need to use modern media in a better way, radio, TV, even Facebook."

She raises some good points, particularly on how much potential there is in better funding for credit unions, not simply as a market player alongside high cost credit, but something that, with political will and social networking know-how, will challenge it as a better deal for consumers. But Chicken's points were not made without reservations for the potential scope for credit unions. "One of the problems for credit unions is the income generated from small short term loans," she said.

As credit unions are the only lenders in Britain which, by law, are obliged to adhere to an interest cap, it can limit the amount of risk they can take on a short-term loan, particularly to a new customer. Sally pointed out: "If we loaned £200 for a month we would earn less than £5 interest. So if we increased our lending to payday loan type borrowers, we would be making ourselves vulnerable to bad payers at the same time as reducing our income." A tricky conversation yet to be had in the credit union movement, is whether it should act upon the findings of the CDFI project My Home Finance that credit unions need to charge 68% interest to cover its costs alone, rather than the current maximum 26.8%.

It's clear that the building up of credit unions has a lot of support from our elected politicians, albeit a support that says there is a long way to go. In the UK, unlike in many other European countries where credit unions are on the corner of every street (in particular Poland), there isn't the same presence. Helen Goodman MP told me that: "Credit unions' coverage is not complete. Alistair Darling did put needed money into them, but they need to be based upon a grander model such as the people's bank, with new entitlements." What exactly those new entitlements could be was something touched upon by Yvonne Forage MP. She opined that credit unions should roll out hole-in-the-wall networks, for which a further investment would be needed. If they did this they could focus on expanding the membership outside of its core target. In short, "credit unions should aim for the best of what the banks have to offer."

Credit unions have the potential to challenge payday lenders. Certainly the boost from the DWP's 2011 £73 million modernisation plan should help, but credit unions need to make sure there is creativity produced from this money. One idea is for credit unions to pursue a home credit service. As the Joseph Rowntree Foundation's report on a not-for-profit home credit product shows, there is a lot of risk inherent to it. Six in 10 customers made a late payment in home credit loans, between 2 and 10 per cent of loans are paid back on time and to contract terms, and between 1 and 6 per cent of loans have no payments made at all. A quality customer, it was assessed, is someone who makes 60 per cent of their repayments on time. On the other hand, people like the convenience of taking out loans from their doorstep, and the market players willing to provide a service like this include home credit sellers like Provident, not to mention the illegal loan sharks. However, if the interest rate of a credit union loan was raised from its current legal setting now, as discussed in the findings of My Home Finance, it gives this plan a fighting chance, and is likely to reach more potential customers as a consequence, and free up the time of volunteers, who seem to spend a disproportionate amount of their time looking for members.

Social enterprises

One person who foresees an alternative to payday lenders, and perceives credit unions to be funded on an outdated model, is Faisal Rahman, the director of Fair Finance, a London-based social enterprise that offers financial products and services designed to meet the needs of people who are financially excluded. The reason that Rahman thinks there is payday growth is because authorised overdrafts are being greatly reduced. He clarifies his own criticism of the APR debate by saying that, looked at it this way, credit unions are less expensive than Fair Finance's product, and there is only really, £1 difference between the price. "Quality of service is the key marker. Not price", Rahman says.

Rahman's distrust of politicians wading in is born not so much out of thinking the market always has it right, but that there is clear lack of empathy there: "It is understandable that politicians have trouble getting to grips with the payday loan market as it is new for them, and they don't have to deal with it like the people in poorer communities."

Politicians might perhaps argue that their link is the electorate that provides knowledge of the market. Instead, it is my opinion that this market has suffered from a severe lack of research, and everyone from politicians to the media to economists assumed that, as only being a small market, it would amount to very little to the economy as a whole. This particular assumption is being challenged, and clearly politicians are waking up to the reality and taking heed of the best of today's focus on that industry.

Rahman says there has been an "abject failure of credit unions." For him, for all but a few it is an unsustainable model that cannot grow, whereas what he has to offer in Fair Finance can. He says that in four years' time Fair Finance will be able to cover its costs without investment, at which point it will be potentially be able to draw profit. Despite his opinion that there are too many strings attached to public money, he thinks that, had all charitable and financial exclusion funding gone into more social enterprise start-ups to price out predators in the market, then this would have provided good value for the government, as opposed to keeping funding credit unions to no avail. "Credit unions are just mobilising the middle class", he says, implying that there is no incentive for credit unions to lend to poorer customers. However, he does admit that there are some bigger credit unions that are very successful, for example, Clockwise in Leicester.

From my own conversations with people who work in credit unions, the reason they don't feel they could compete for the low-income earner to lend at reasonable prices is not because they don't believe, but because they spend too much time fighting for funding than targeting new members. For all the money being pumped into credit unions there is still nothing in the kitty for advertising – and as Nic Daikin MP put it bluntly, "credit unions are invisible to the person on the street". This is the crucial problem.

After all, private money is not any less risky as Rahman found out himself. It was reported at the time that Fair Finance was declined investment money by Barclays and the Royal Bank of Scotland. When asked about it, he did say it was a setback, and they even had problems with Santander which would not invest alone. This is not the fault of Fair Finance. Their model of lending to the home credit market is risky for investors. While his understanding of the risk is very sophisticated, and his heart is in the right place, he and the organisation found out themselves that when the market is rocky, borrowing for growing a business is not easy.

Providing reasonable loans with public money often requires political will, and with consideration to the long-term cost impact, early intervention, though seemingly expensive in the short term, is often most sensible. But, without casting too many aspersions on banks and their lending practices, it is often less about will, and more about how risky it seems, and whether the return will be the one they want. Having less commitment to the wider world, as has been continuously proven with excessive pay packets and undue bonuses, banks don't have to invest just because there is an urgent need to make sure poor people don't get poorer. It is for this reason that I don't necessarily share Rahman's optimism that social enterprises, through private equity help, should be the only player in town, accumulating those funding streams originally designed for CDFI projects and credit unions. The risks of not getting that investment seem too high, and unfortunately the good-hearted Rahman has to rely on that investment before he can run without it, reinvesting profit himself back into the social enterprise.

Microfinance

One of the models that Rahman is most influenced by, is the microfinance movement. The microfinance movement began in the early 1970s in Bangladesh and Latin America and since then has seen small but effective support around the world. One of the modern outcomes of this movement is Self-Financed Communities (SFCs). On the subject of SFCs, Salomon Raydan Rivas, whose book 'The Other Microfinance' was published on Kindle in 2011, told me that the majority of worldwide financial transactions do not occur from big institutions or organised institutions at all, rather, from informal mechanisms. This seems like common sense when we consider lending money between friends or families, but what is it that explains this counterfactual? It is not quite explained by him, but perhaps this is understandable. Indeed, not even Professor Mohammed Yunnus, the don of microfinance understood this, he told me. Yunus "developed a banking model to help prevent usuries and speculators from taking advantage of the poor. But he lacked the understanding of local mechanisms already used by thousands of people that effectively combine savings and credit and reduce the costs that users pay for financial services." What Saloman and others want to do now is not formalise these mechanisms, but join them up and give them a stability that can better ensure their longevity, since he ultimately believes this to be good for financial block-building. In his words, his work is around creating a "much simpler [system, one] more directly beneficial for users."

Part of the crisis in microfinace in India, he says, is that it can leave people more indebted. This is a resounding problem. What is often the case is that "formal institutions struggle to meet the poor's financial needs at reasonable costs. Rising interest rates charged for loans are a clear reflection of this problem." The instinct here might be to utilise more formal financial tools. Not for Saloman. He says: "The effort to formally 'bank' the poor is unnecessary." But the designs go further. "If we convert the informal mechanisms into safer and more efficient instruments", he says, "then the poor will have access to quality basic financial services –without the need to go through the complexity involved in the formal banking system." So though there are no plans to compete with banks, there is also the opinion that banks will never be able to cater for a certain type of person. Something shared by payday lenders for example, perhaps even shared by banks themselves.

The notion that SFCs are not competing with banks was also raised by by David Shurjin, who said: "An SFC will not provide you a loan for buying a house, for example, but it becomes really useful for everyone in a day-to-day economy." The SFC is focused on people that do not have formal access to main-stream credit and are therefore relevant to our discussion. But it seems to me that the scope for what David and others are trying to do is already encapsulated in the work of mutually-owned credit unions and that small informal groupings, while very good in localities, are inevitably going to face those same problems that mutuals are up against themselves. SFCs may well one day be the beneficiaries of committed funding from community development money, but the task to secure money for existing credit unions is hard enough, let alone the operational difficulties of joining them up and saving on other costs (such as the staffing time spent looking for members rather than focusing on the existing ones and lending to clients who would otherwise fall into the traps of loan sharks, legal or illegal).

Re-energising the credit union

These types of financial interventions should not be competing with each other. What I would prefer to see, rather than Faisel Rahman saying credit unions are stuck on an ineffective model, is some of his noble ideas being fed into a modernised credit union model. There have been plenty of attempts at re-energising credit unions, and the temptation is to write them off, saying that they'll never compete. This is what John Spriggs of the Staffordshire Credit Union told me. "Credit unions aren't a viable option for a lot of people. If you need £200 this week and the bank won't do you an overdraft, there needs to be that gap filled. Credit unions just cannot fill that gap." But European case studies tell us different. Even examples from the UK show that credit unions are in a position to lend in competition to high cost lenders on the high street or online. These credit unions, however, tend to be the ones with long-term funding or that are linked up regionally. Stella Creasy MP told me that it would be a "generation or more before credit unions would fill in the gap that payday lenders occupy." This is undeniably true, and this is why credit unions should be listening to the likes of Rahman.

There is the assumption that if more people only knew about credit unions everything would be better. That's partially true. One third of the adults in Ireland are members of a credit union, and even though Ireland has only 50 more credit unions nationally than Britain as a whole, it has two million more members. I'm sure one way to solve this problem is with more dedicated advertising and awareness. Funding is also a problem. One credit union staff member in the North of England told me that the credit union he works for is operating on two years' allocated funding, with other staff, mainly volunteers, spending their time trying to secure more funding and inviting other members along – in the knowledge that only a minority of those members will be *active* members. Down the road, a bigger credit union has 10 years' funding to play with, meaning that they can pool a greater proportion of their time getting members, rather than focusing on short term funding problems. This makes all the difference. It doesn't take a genius to work out which of the two has the greater means to lend short term and undercut the payday lenders.

CHAPTER 7
CONCLUSION

IF PAYDAY LOANS were used as a means to settle a single unexpected bill over a few days or get a forgotten family friend a birthday present, then there is a very little fuss we could kick up about their existence. Sure, you'd be paying through the nose, and you'd surely wonder why there wasn't any alternative available from the state or a small local enterprise, but if you borrowed the cash, purchased or paid back what you needed and then paid off the loan you would probably leave it there and make no more bones about it. The problem is that this rarely happens.

The reason payday lenders have seen recent growth and a rise in their so-called 'target audience' is because people are struggling, banks are failing to lend out and wages are losing the battle against inflation, despite living in the country with the longest working hours in Europe. People are clearly cutting back on spending but still face an uphill challenge, and with job losses and subdued growth forecast for the next five years if not longer, it's no wonder people are doing self-defeating things such as borrowing from payday lenders.

Why not ban the payday lenders?

So why not ban payday lenders?

A 2011 Management Information Service report which sought to determine what a 'reasonable' level of expenditure is, found that borrowing from high and very high cost credit lenders is likely to significantly reduce the living standards of low income households and may not therefore be affordable. Surely the solution is simple – just close them down! If only. The solution should be made through pricing out the industry in other ways, not aggressively closing its network down – this doesn't solve the real problem, or the *causes* of the problem of payday lenders. If we look at the financial and economic land-scape today we start to understand that there is a way to go, and the long-term solution isn't banning things.

With debt advice services, at a time when they are needed the most, the government seems intent on making life harder for them. On 6 March 2012 the Citizen's Advice Bureau announced that legal aid cuts would make it almost impossible for it to carry on providing specialist advice. Andrew Penman, commenting on this for the *Mirror* was far more scathing: "So the Tory-led government has decided to take an axe to the UK's Citizens Advice bureaux network, leaving the needy at the mercy of an industry awash with shysters just when they badly need free and impartial debt advice."[94]

High debt, with the squeezed budgets of those who can help individuals out with them, has unhelpfully emerged at a time when people have historically low savings. As mentioned earlier, 70 per cent of the poorest children live in households that cannot afford to save £10 a week, or take a week's holiday away from home once a year. Asked whether this government was putting a strain on personal savings, the anonymous blog-ger Left Outside told me that "personal savings do seem to be under strain as people bring forward consumption while times are bad ... if more people save this reduces demand, as economic orthodoxy tends to put it, but reducing the extent to which low income households can save, even modestly, risks exposing them to 'shocks' and increases the chances of them using legal loan sharks or even unlicensed lenders."

A report by the Resolution Foundation pointed out that now in recessionary times (double-dip recession to be precise) households in Britain are experiencing a fall in the buying power of their income. The authors continue:

> "A combination of falling real earnings, falling government support and substantial rises in the cost of items from food to petrol and household energy are hitting the living standards of people across the income spectrum, with the Institute for Fiscal Studies estimating that real household incomes fell 3.5 per cent last year."[95]

Unemployment and underemployment

Even where jobs are stable and wages are coming in on a regular basis, their worth is dropping rapidly.

The Living Wage is defined as the minimum income amount a professional can receive to provide them and their families the essentials they need in life. 5 million workers in the UK – 20 per cent of the total number of employees – earn less than the living wage and employees in the South East, the North West and London all have more than half a million people earning less than the living wage. While inequality is as high today as it has been at any time in the previous three decades, the top decile, assessed by income, accounts for 30 per cent of all income. The bottom decile accounts for just 1 per cent.

In April 2012, the coalition government had been celebrating some signs that unemployment had dropped for the first time since May 2011. But this was only hiding a deeper problem which has been brewing up since the UK credit crunch – that of 'underemployment'. It has been cited by the Office for National Statistics (ONS) that 1,418,000 people are in a position where they are working too few hours because that's all they can find. Underemployment includes people doing part-time jobs, temporary jobs or shifts where they can, because something is better than nothing. In some cases, clearly, nothing is better than something, particularly where work, as the familiar saying today goes, doesn't pay. Often for these people, being on benefits would mean more stability, but the worry about gaps on CVs and how that could affect future job prospects incentivises, at best, a modest income to cover overheads. At worst, these workers can be defined as the working poor.

The estimates are that 2 million people can be defined as underemployed, when you factor in other estimates such as the number now self-employed (on the assumption that not all of those who are now self-employed are getting much work, who, rather, have been pushed out of 'paid work and are forced to go it alone' – the ONS does not ask the self-employed if they would rather be working as an employee). The TUC has pointed out that the figure could be somewhat higher than that. As the Big Innovation Centre researcher Andrew Sissons says, this is on top of the 2.6 million people who are officially counted as unemployed.[96]

U-turns on middle-class mothers losing their child benefit, cutting low-income individuals out of tax and keeping interest rates down to bring mortgage prices down are just some of the things that the government talk about to show that their time in office hasn't been a complete mess. But even if you buy this, and forget the array of other interventions and financial disasters (such as plummeting jobs, low and no growth coupled with tax breaks for the wealthy) since May 2010 that have bolstered the squeeze, these small moves are not, as they paint it themselves, putting money back in the pockets of hard working families and those feeling the pinch during the recession. This doesn't go anywhere near putting money back. This is symbolism. This is like pillaging a farmer's autumn crop and giving him a few berries back, saying here we are putting food on his family's plate. Of course, we can't only blame the current administration for this.

Housing costs and fuel poverty

Research from the Joseph Rowntree Foundation found that in 2008/09, households in the bottom fifth of the income distribution spent an average of 30 per cent of their disposable income on housing itself. Overall households, both private and social, in the bottom fifth spend a greater proportion of their income on housing costs. This is without mentioning fuel poverty. The Warm House Discount is a new scheme funded by energy suppliers which came into force in April 2011 that will bring £1.13 billion in direct and indirect financial support to vulnerable consumers over the next four years. The discount is divided into core group (pensioners) and broad group (anyone else who feels they are eligible, who are asked to apply). But Save the Children, though broadly supportive of the scheme in principle, worry that if it isn't widened out further, could risk failing to achieve the main goal which is reducing fuel poverty. One of Save the Children's recommendations for the scheme is for the core and broad groups to be merged and the core group to be expanded to include families in receipt of the Child Tax Credit up to the first income threshold of £16,190.

On housing itself, the details are very depressing. The Resolution Foundation's report on housing pointed out that: "It would have taken the average low-to-middle income household 31 years to accumulate a deposit for the average first home if they saved 5 per cent of their income each year and had no access to the 'bank of Mum and Dad'".[97] On top of this, social housing has failed to accommodate for need. When Prime Minister Thatcher came to power the UK had 5.3 million social homes – today there are 3.7 million. Private renting hasn't been made any easier. As author and journalist Owen Jones put it, from his own experience, "Looking for a modest two-bedroom place in London's Zone 2, I found that a standard monthly individual rent was £800, even £900. One estate agent asked what our maximum budget was: when I suggested £700 each a month, he spluttered down the phone."[98]

In April 2012 Newham Council was accused of 'social cleansing' for its plans to move families claiming housing benefit to other parts of the country, such as Stoke-on-Trent. It was revealed by Newham Mayor Sir Robin Wales that the Council wrote to more than 1,100 organisations to try to move families on after it admitted it could not afford to have them stay in their current abodes. The MP for Stoke Central, Tristram Hunt, said the area did not need "difficult-to-house cases", but on top of this is the issue of whether it is right and ethical to move a family from its home. The contention might be that governments who are paying out benefit have the legal right to take the place where that money is going away, but is it fair? Not only that, is it sensible? After all housing stability is helpful towards finding work – and any help is needed. Moving vulnerable families who are out of work into an area where there is even less work is not only bad planning, but risks increasing community tension.

But there are already stories where people are being priced out right now, that the media tends not to focus on at all. A single mother I have spoken to in Brent, has had to change the nursery her daughter goes to because of the cut to how much money she was afforded by the local authority. Unable to afford the costs by herself, she was forced to seek an alternative. To make matters worse, the cut to her housing benefit has meant she is priced out of the area she has lived in for most of her life, and all of her life as a mother. She told me that she doesn't have very long to move out because she has no chance of affording the costs with her income alone. The chances of her finding somewhere within Zones 2-3 in London are slim, which means more messing about with different nurseries for her child. What has since been termed the 'social cleansing' of Newham has been happening around London all along.

Lack of financial education

Rod McKee, a Vice Principal at the IFS School for Finance, told me that when he visits schools he is often stunned at how little is known or is taught about personal finance, even from an early age. He said: "I visited a school in Hackney earlier this year, when we set the students a task of researching financial terms on the internet the only one they didn't need to look up was loan shark! I do not know if this was because of what they see on television or from local knowledge, although my impression was it was the latter." This is a shocking indictment, and one that is clearly only set to increase.

The IFS is currently the only specialist provider of GCSE, AS and A level equivalent qualifications in personal finance and financial studies. This should give us pause. At the moment, financial education in schools is lacking severely, often to the point where teachers are having to create lessons on this from scratch without there being a proper curriculum on this to work from. The Money Saving Expert Martin Lewis said, as part of his written evidence to the All Party Parliamentary Group on Financial Education for Young People to inform the inquiry into Financial Education and the Curriculum, that it is a "national disgrace that for over 20 years in the UK we have educated our youth into debt when they go to university, but never educated them about debt."

It's not going to solve the problem of bad debt, nor of payday loans, alone, but it is a start, and might give us some idea of why there is a big personal debt problem today. As McKee went on to say:

> "If we have students who have good financial education they would be able to question why anyone would want to borrow at such high rates of interest and how they can justify such rates. What we need are educated consumers that are aware of what they are taking on. Whereas at the moment it is the poor, the desperate and the uninformed

who always end with the highest rates of interest charged and they are the ones who can afford it least."

Financial education, alongside better regulation on predatory lenders, sensible policies to reduce income inequality could really have a positive effect on the finances of the most vulnerable in society, and beyond.

Conclusions

My conclusions are as follows:

- People have fought, along class lines, long and hard to enjoy access to credit, even if it is to enter into the world of consumer capitalism. We might apply modern-day appeals to commodity fetishism, but as research into the riots has shown, consumerism is deeply embedded into modern society. What I conclude about consumerism is that high-society has often frowned upon credit for the poor on the grounds that it shows financial imprudence. The argument still exists today. We need to counter that, not on grounds of right, but to say there is a duty to provide for those lesser off in society in lieu of fairer deals on wages, while also reminding politicians and businesses that credit should never be an alternative to better pay deals and working conditions. In short, we should accept credit as a marker of a healthy economy, but we should not be complacent about what it often replaces.

- With bank risk aversion and the prospect that as much as 43 per cent of British households have experienced financial difficulties with their household bills or credit commitments at some time in the past 12 months, we risk handing a lot of people over to the high cost credit market. Banks should, as part of their obligation towards wider society, offer emergency overdrafts for

124

people on low incomes to be used when experiencing financial shocks. In many other countries this is a very uncontroversial practice, but seems to be a common sense approach too far in the UK.

- Whether there should be a definite cap on the amount of times a person rolls over on a loan is one question, but this intervention would be nothing were it not matched with a period of tailored financial advice and a suitable debt repayment programme, inclusive of cooling-off periods, as well as a referral to a local credit union. This would necessitate stronger, more pro-active regulation of the type that the new FCA should be thinking about adopting, and could be facilitated by something like the Veritac system, if not this system itself, to flag up those individuals who reach a maximum amount of loans taken before appropriate financial action should be sought.

- The social fund should be immediately reinstated and centralised, with reform that would allow the government to cope better with lending to low income families in times of financial shock. Policy makers should consider making the social fund something that operates through a credit union, which would increase a credit union's funding and do more to highlight its social importance.

- Policy makers should also seriously consider making good on Veronika Thiel's recommendation in her report 'Doorstep Robbery' the creation of a community reinvestment act which would see banks not lending sufficiently in local communities obliged to sponsor local affordable lenders such as credit unions.

It is apparent that problems of high bad debt at the hands of payday lenders will not solve itself. Arch free market advocates have accepted that. But it is incumbent upon elected representatives to make the proactive reforms, some of which I hope to have addressed above, in order that a real change is made for families and households in Britain.

However, stronger moves against payday lenders cannot be an option in isolation. After all, the notion that payday lenders have increased their operations since the financial recession should tell us that they are a symptom of the problem. However, they are also the cause of the continuation of the problem. Their business models rely on returning customers. Just as John Lamidey of the Consumer Finance Association has admitted, it makes perfect sense to have repeat borrowers "as it does if you shop at Marks and Spencers [sic]". The government must set about a radical, and integrated, plan to tackle the causes and the problems of payday lender success, at the expense of those who can least afford it, and it must not wait another moment to do so.

A *Guardian* article on May 18, 2012, as double-dip recession was filtering through the news stations, pointed out that: "Almost two-thirds of people who took out expensive payday loans have used the money to pay household bills or buy essentials such as food, nappies and petrol, a survey by Which? has revealed."

These stories, about real people who we encounter every day, are not stories about problems, but crises.[99]

ENDNOTES

i   http://blogs.telegraph.co.uk/news/brendanoneill2/100234383/the-crusade-against-wonga-is-in-danger-of-resurrecting-the-stereotype-of-the-avaricious-jewish-moneylender/
ii http://www.thisismoney.co.uk/money/bills/article-2065563/Skipton-survey-claims-average-family-needs-25-000-year-pay-bills-buy-basics.html
iii www.thefsforum.co.uk/.../ChangingGeographyofBranchnetworks.pdf
iv http://www.pwc.co.uk/financial-services/publications/precious-plastic-2012.jhtml
v   http://yougov.co.uk/news/2013/07/31/welbys-challenge-highlights-how-vulnerable-wonga/
vii http://www.dailyrecord.co.uk/news/scottish-news/revealed-scots-boss-payday-loan-2240215
vii http://politicalscrapbook.net/2013/06/payday-loan-firm-slammed-over-fake-social-life-text-messages/
viii http://www.bris.ac.uk/geography/research/pfrc/themes/credit-debt/total-cost-of-credit.html
ix http://www.fca.org.uk/your-fca/documents/occasional-papers/occasional-paper-1
x   http://www.credittoday.co.uk/article/14932/online-news/wonga-responds-to-ofts-payday-report
xi http://www.thisismoney.co.uk/money/cardsloans/article-2317239/Wonga-raids-15-year-olds-bank-account-recover-debts-BBC-Watchdog.html
xii http://www.thisismoney.co.uk/money/cardsloans/article-2292044/Wonga-leaves-dozens-victims-answers-raids-bank-accounts-30-000-recover-loans-fraudsters.html
xiii http://www.newstatesman.com/politics/2013/06/osborne-hits-unemployed-and-poor-students
xiv https://twitter.com/paullewismoney/status/345096223864274944
xv http://www.totalpolitics.com/articles/384457/archbishopand39s-move-can-welby-restore-faith-in-the-church.thtml
xvi http://www.telegraph.co.uk/news/religion/10206098/Justin-Welbys-Wonga-revelation.html#comment-978949727
xvii http://www.ft.com/cms/s/0/1855c6bc-f544-11e2-b4f8-00144feabdc0.html
xviii http://www.telegraph.co.uk/news/religion/9700796/Justin-Welby-the-Bishop-of-Durham-calls-for-cap-on-total-cost-of-payday-loans.html

1   Jill Insley, "Payday lenders charge up to 60 times more than true cost of loan", *Guardian*, December 7, 2011. Accessed August 25, 2012. http://www.guardian. co.uk/money/2011/dec/07/payday-lenders-loans-cost

2   R3, "Rein in 'payday lenders', say 93% of GB population", May 22, 2012. Accessed August 25, 2012. http://www.r3.org.uk/index.cfm?page=1114&element=16322

3   Paul Routledge, "Advance of payday lenders is a dismal sign of the times" *Daily Mirror*, March 9, 2012. Accessed August 25, 2012. http://www.mirror.co.uk/news/ uk-news/advance-of-payday-lenders-is-a-dismal-sign-756020

4   Rosa-Maria Gelpi and François Julien-Labruyère, The History of Consumer Credit: Doctrines and Practice, UK: Palgrave Macmillan, 2000

5   Michael Hudson, "The New Economic Archaeology of Debt", http://michael-hudson.com/, April 23, 2002. Accessed May 18, 2012. http://michael-hudson. com/2002/04/the-new-economic-archaeology-of-debt/

6   David Graeber, Debt: The First 5000 Years, UK: Melville House Publishing, 2011

7   ibid

8   Lendol G Calder, "The History of Consumer Credit: Doctrines and Practices", *Economic History Association*, August 24, 2000. Accessed August 25, 2012. http:// eh.net/book_reviews/history-consumer-credit-doctrines-and-practices

9   Constant J. Mews and Ibrahim Abraham, "Usury and Just Compensation: Religious and Financial Ethics in Historical Perspective", Journal of Business Ethics, Vol. 72, No. 1 (Apr., 2007)

10 Stephen James, "The ancient evil of usury", *News Review*, July 19, 2001. Accessed May 18, 2012. http://www.newsreview.com/sacramento/ancient-evil-of-usury/ content?oid=7610

11 ibid

12 As Donna M. Kish-Goodling once put it, on the subject of *The Merchant of Venice* and the teaching of monetary economics, "Often literary works reflect our economic life more accurately than today's economic statistical techniques and mathematical models")

13 Amanda Bailey, "Shylock and the Slaves: Owing and Owning in The Merchant of Venice", *Shakespeare Quarterly*, Vol. 62, No. 1 (January 2011)

14 Roya Nikkah, "New book claims Robin Hood stole from the rich and lent to the poor", *Telegraph*, March 6, 2010. Accessed May 18, 2012. http://www.telegraph. co.uk/culture/books/booknews/7385198/New-book-claims-Robin-Hood-stole-from-the-rich-and-lent-to-the-poor.html

15 Frank Trentmann, "Beyond Consumerism: New Historical Perspectives on Consumption", Journal of Contemporary History, Vol. 39, No. 3 (Jul., 2004)

16 Margot Finn, The Character of Credit: Personal Debt in English Culture, 1740–1914, UK: Cambridge University Press, 2003

17 Paul Johnson, Credit, Debtors and the Law in Victorian and Edwardian England, based on a paper prepared for a conference on 'Private Law and Social Inequality in the Industrial Age' held at the German Historical Institute, London, 14-17 December 1995.

18 Max Horkheimer and Theodor Adorno, *Dialectic of Enlightenment*, US: Standford University Press, 2003 (1947)

19 Michael Billig, "Commodity Fetishism and Repression: Reflections on Marx, Freud and the Psychology of Consumer Capitalism," Theory & Psychology, vol. 9 no. 3, 1999

20 Thorstein Veblen, *The Theory of the Leisure Class*, UK: Dover Publications Inc., 1994 (1899)

21 Richard Elliot et al, "Man Management? Women and the Use of Debt to Control Personal Relationships," Journal of Marketing Management, vol. 12 no. 7, 1996

22 The Guardian/London School of Economics, Reading the Riots: Investigating England's summer of disorder, 2011

23 Orazio P. Attanasio and Gugliemo Weber, "The UK consumption boom of the late 1980s: aggregate implications of microeconomic evidence," The Economic Journal, vol. 104 no. 427, 1994

24 Lyn Thomas et al, "A survey of the issues in consumer credit modelling research," Journal of the Operational Research Society, vol 56 no. 9, 2005

25 Price Waterhouse Coopers, Precious Plastic: All change please, 2012

26 Veronika Thiel, Doorstep Robbery: Why the UK needs a fair lending law, The New Economics Foundation, 2009

27 Consumer Focus/University of Bristol Personal Finance Research Centre, Affordable credit: Lessons from overseas, 2011

28 Stephen Jenkins, *Changing fortunes: income mobility and poverty dynamics in Britain*, UK: Oxford University Press, 2011

29 Sophie Parker, Behind the balance sheet: the financial health of low earning households, Resolution Foundation, 2010

30 Hannah Aldridge, Anushree Parekh, Tom MacInnes and Peter Kenway, Monitoring poverty and social exclusion 2011, Joseph Rowntree Foundation, 2011

31 Dalia Ben-Galim, Asset stripping: Child Trust Funds and the demise of the assets agenda, ippr, 2011

32 Larry Elliott, "Paying off your debts hits the economy, stupid", Guardian, October 5, 2011. Accessed April 17, 2012. http://www.guardian.co.uk/business/2011/oct/05/david-cameron-paradox-of-thrift

33 Kevin Gulliver & John Morris, Living on the Edge: Financial Exclusion & Social Housing, The Human City Institute, 2011

34 Damian Kahya, "Fuel poverty to rise to 8.5m, report warns", BBC News, March 15, 2012. Accessed April 17, 2012. http://www.bbc.co.uk/news/business-17365137

35 Stewart Lansley, *The Cost of Inequality: Three Decades of the Super-Rich and the Economy*, UK: Gibson Square Books Ltd., 2011

36 Paul Jones, Access to Credit on a Low Income, a study into how people on low incomes in Liverpool access and use consumer credit, The Co-operative Bank, 2001

37 Faisal Rahman, "High-cost lenders are cashing in on spending review cuts", *Guardian*, October 27, 2010, http://www.guardian.co.uk/society/2010/oct/27/high-cost-lenders-spending-review-cuts

38 Transitioning high risk low income borrowers to affordable credit, Policis, 2011.

39 Henry Palmer and Pat Conaty, Profiting from Poverty: Why debt is big business in Britain, The New Economics Foundation, 2003

40 Grant Shapps, "Pay- Day for Loan Sharks: How the poorest in society are paying up to10,000 % APR as the Bank of England slashes its lending rate towards zero", http://www.shapps.com/reports/PayDay-for-Loan-Sharks.pdf

41 Veronika Thiel, Doorstep Robbery: Why the UK needs a fair lending law, The New Economics Foundation, 2009

42 Karen Rowlingson and Elaine Kempson, Moneylenders and their customers, Policy Studies Institute, 1994

43 Elaine Kempson, Anna Ellison, Claire Whyley and Paul Jones, Is a not-for-profit home credit business feasible, Joseph Rowntree Foundation, 2009

44 Edward M. Lewis, *An Introduction to Credit Scoring*, UK: Athena Press, 1994

45 Richard Wachman, "Pawnbrokers' efforts to shed Dickensian image suffer setback as OFT moves in", Guardian, February 26, 2012, http://www.guardian.co.uk/money/2012/feb/26/pawnbrokers-payday-loans-oft-inquiry

46 Chris Leslie and Alex Hood, Circling the Loan Sharks: Predatory lending in the recession and the emerging role for local government, New Local Government Network, 2009

47 Sharon Collard and David Hayes, Pawnbroking Customers in 2010: A Survey (A report to the National Pawnbrokers Association), Personal Finance Research Centre, University of Bristol, 2010

48 Polly Toynbee, *Hard Work*, UK: Bloomsbury, 2003

49 Jane Moore, "£100 loan has cost me £2400", The Sun, December 9, 2009. Accessed April 6, 2012. http://www.thesun.co.uk/sol/homepage/features/2760675/The-peril-of-easy-credit-at-Christmas.html

50 Michael A. Stegman, "Payday Lending," *The Journal of Economic Perspectives*, Vol. 21, No. 1 (Winter, 2007)

51 Mark J. Flannery and Katherine Samolyk, "Payday Lending: Do the Costs Justify the Price?" *FDIC Center for Financial Research Working Paper*, No. 2005/09 (June 2005). Available at SSRN: http://ssrn.com/abstract=771624 or http://dx.doi.org/10.2139/ssrn.771624

52 Sarah O'Connor, "Payday sector in search of new frontier," Financial Times, December 11, 2011. Accessed April 6, 2012. http://www.ft.com/cms/s/0/e52da39e-2011-11e1-8462-00144feabdc0.html#axzz1rGqBjUGd

53 Tim Harford, "Is payday lending really wrong?" Tim Harford: *The Undercover Economist*, December 10, 2011. Accessed April 6, 2012. http://timharford.com/2011/12/is-payday-lending-really-wrong/

54 Marie Burton, Keeping the plates spinning: perceptions of payday loans in Great Britain, Consumer Focus, 2010

55 Money Advice Trust and University of Bristol Personal Finance Research Centre, Understanding financial difficulty: Exploring the opportunities for early intervention, 2011

56 Shelter, "Millions rely on credit to pay for home," March 9, 2012. Accessed April 6, 2012. http://england.shelter.org.uk/news/january_2012/millions_rely_on_credit_to_pay_for_home

57 R3, "Personal Debt Snapshot: 'Zombie' debtors emerge" November 2011. Accessed April 11, 2012.

58 Mark J. Flannery and Katherine Samolyk, "Payday Lending: Do the Costs Justify the Price?" *FDIC Center for Financial Research Working Paper*, No. 2005/09 (June 2005). Available at SSRN: http://ssrn.com/abstract=771624 or http://dx.doi.org/10.2139/ssrn.771624

59 Nikki Watkins, "Borrowing £550 cost me £3k to pay back... I ended up broke and homeless", *The Sun*, January 10, 2012. Accessed April 11, 2012. http://www.thesun.co.uk/sol/homepage/woman/real_life/4049358/Borrowing-550-cost-me-3k-to-pay-back-I-ended-up-broke-and-homeless.html

60 See http://saynotopaydayloans.co.uk/

61 Rosie Murray-West, "Legal loansharks are targeting the military, warns MP for Walthamstow Stella Creasy", *Telegraph*, November 11, 2011. Accessed April 26, 2012. http://www.telegraph.co.uk/finance/personalfinance/borrowing/8884178/Legal-loansharks-are-targeting-the-military-warns-MP-for-Walthamstow-Stella-Creas.html

62 Elizabeth Rigby, "About 1m take out payday loans", *Financial Times*, January 3, 2012. Accessed April 26, 2012. www.ft.com/cms/s/0/6c4889d6-363b-11e1-a3fa-00144feabdc0.html

63 Sharlene Goff, "Crisis boosts growth in payday loans sector", *Financial Times*, December 6, 2011. Accessed April 26, 2012. http://www.ft.com/cms/s/0/fc906960-2019-11e1-8462-00144feabdc0.html#axzz1tB8JfgRu

64 Elaine Moore, "Credit unions benefit from rule changes", *Financial Times*, January 9, 2012. Accessed April 26, 2012. http://www.ft.com/cms/s/0/0c3fceba-3acc-11e1-a756-00144feabdc0.html

65 Becky Barrow, "Britain has become 'wild west' for payday loan lenders with millions at risk of losing their homes, MPs warn", *Daily Mail*, March 7, 2012. Accessed April 26, 2012. Britain has become 'wild west' for payday loan lenders with millions at risk of losing their homes, MPs warn

66 Vanessa Allen, 'Pay-day' loans used to fund plastic surgery: Website deals linked to 'good looks', Daily Mail, February 5, 2012. Accessed April 26, 2012. http://www.dailymail.co.uk/news/article-2096956/Pay-day-loans-used-fund-plastic-surgery-Website-deals-linked-good-looks.html

67 Ruth Lythe, "How women are being seduced into debt by payday parasites: 'Instant' cash firms with interest rates as high as 16,000% are ruining lives", *Daily Mail*, January 31, 2012. Accessed April 26, 2012. http://www.dailymail.co.uk/news/article-2094115/Instant-money-loans-Payday-loan-firms-ruining-lives.html

68 Nick Sommerlad, "This won't hurt a bit, says payday lender Toothfairy Finance", *Daily Mirror*, September 21, 2012. Accessed April 26, 2012. http://blogs.mirror.co.uk/investigations/2011/09/this-wont-hurt-a-bit-says-payd.html

69 See the Consumer Action Group forum titled "Toothfairy Finance – I need help" http://www.consumeractiongroup.co.uk/forum/showthread.php?196995-Toothfairy-Finance-I-Need-Help

70 William Shaw, "Cash machine: Could Wonga transform personal finance?", *Wired Magazine*, May 5, 2011. Accessed April 11, 2012. http://www.wired.co.uk/magazine/archive/2011/06/features/wonga?page=all

71 Amelia Gentleman, "Wonga: the real cost of a payday loan", *Guardian*, March 1, 2012. Accessed April 11, 2012. http://www.guardian.co.uk/business/2012/mar/01/wonga-real-cost-payday-loan

72 Alex Hern, "Wonga target students with friendly advice: Take our 4000% loan", *Left Foot Forward*, January 11, 2012. Accessed April 11, 2012. http://www.leftfootforward.org/2012/01/wonga-target-students-with-friendly-advice-take-our-4000-loan/

73 Alan O'Sullivan, "Payday loans: Wonga, best of a bad bunch?", *This is Money*, May 17, 2010. Accessed April 11, 2012. http://www.thisismoney.co.uk/money/cardsloans/article-1677524/Payday-loans-Wonga-best-of-a-bad-bunch.html

74 KeyNote Market Assessment, (2005) 'Financial Services Organisations on the Internet', 3rd Edition (July 2005).

75 SM Finlay, "Predictive models of expenditure and over-indebtedness for assessing the affordability of new consumer credit applications", Journal of the Operational Research Society, 57, 655-696

76 Anna Ellison and Robert Forster, The impact of interest rate ceilings: The evidence from international experience and the implications for regulation and consumer protection in the credit market in Australia, Policis, 2008.

77 Jane Perry, Paying over the odds? Real-life experiences of the poverty premium, Church Action on Poverty, 2010.

78 Carl Packman, "Loosening the grip of legal loan sharks", *Guardian*, November 14, 2010. Accessed April 11, 2012. http://www.guardian.co.uk/commentisfree/2010/nov/14/loan-sharks-consumer-credit-bill

79 Richard Murphy, The case for an interest rate cap in the UK: A study based on Provident Financial plc, Church Action on Poverty, The New Economics Foundation and Debt on our Doorstep, 2003.

80 Hilary Osborne, "Personal insolvencies at three-year low", *Guardian*, February 3, 2012. Accessed April 11, 2012. http://www.guardian.co.uk/money/2012/feb/03/personal-insolvency-three-year-low

81 Matthew Whittaker, Squeezed Britain: low-to-middle earners audit 2010, The Resolution Foundation, November 2010.

82 Sharon Collard, Facing the squeeze: a qualitative study of household finances and access to credit in a 21st century recession, University of Bristol Personal Finance Research Centre, 2009.

83 Anna Adams, "The loan sharks who prowl Britain's estates", *BBC News*, Febraury 15, 2012. Accessed May 18, 2012. http://www.bbc.co.uk/news/uk-17041062

84 Karen Rowlingson and Elaine Kempson, Moneylenders and their customers, Policy Studies Institute, 1994

85 Paul Jones, Access to Credit on a Low Income, a study into how people on low incomes in Liverpool access and use consumer credit, The Co-operative Bank, 2001

86 Staff writer, "Money lending team looks to hunt down loan sharks", *North-West Evening Mail*, February 11, 2012. Accessed May 18, 2012. http://www.nwemail.co.uk/news/money-lending-team-looks-to-hunt-down-loan-sharks-1.808078?referrerPath=home

87 Staff writer, "Loan shark made £500,000' from Sri Lankan community", *BBC News*, March 14, 2011. Accessed May 18, 2012. http://www.bbc.co.uk/news/uk-england-london-12736957

88 Daily Mail reporter, "Ex-boxing champion turned loan shark ordered to pay back over £260k in illegal gains", *Daily Mail*, March 5, 2011. Accessed May 18, 2012. http://www.dailymail.co.uk/news/article-1363289/Ex-boxing-champion-turned-loan-shark-Michael-Morris-ordered-pay-260k-illegal-gains.html

89 Policis, Evaluation of the illegal moneylending pilots, PFRC and Policis, 2007

90 Neal Lawson and Zoe Gannon, Banks We Can Believe In, Compass, 2010

91 Timothy W. Guinnane, "Cooperatives as Information Machines: German Rural Credit Cooperatives, 1883-1914", *The Journal of Economic History*, Vol. 61, No. 2 (Jun., 2001)

92 A credit union working paper found here http://www.creditunionresearch.com/uploads/workingpaper1

93 Paul Jones, "Credit Union and CDFI Training and Development Needs Analysis", Department of Work and Pensions, 2007

94 Andrew Penman, "Swindler's List: the debt and loan sharks that deserve credit crunching", *Daily Mirror*, February 9, 2011. Accessed May 18, 2012. http://blogs.mirror.co.uk/investigations/2011/02/swindlers-list-the-debt-and-lo.html

95 Donald Hirsch, Priced Out, Resolution Foundation, 2011

96 Andrew Sissons, "Unemployment and Underemployment - How Much Pain has the Recession Really Caused?", *Huffington Post*, April 18, 2012. Accessed May 18, 2012. http://www.huffingtonpost.co.uk/andrew-sissons/unemployment-figures_b_1434107.html

97 Matthew Whittaker, The Essential Guide to Squeezed Britain, Resolution Foundation, 2012

98 Owen Jones, "I can afford to pay the rent – most people can't", *Independent*, April 20, 2012. Accessed May 18, 2012. http://www.independent.co.uk/opinion/commentators/owen-jones-i-can-afford-to-pay-the-rent--most-people-cant-7661562.html

99 Jill Insley, "Payday loan borrowers 'trapped in debt spiral'", *Guardian*, May 18, 2012. Accessed May 18, 2012. http://www.guardian.co.uk/money/2012/may/18/payday-loan-borrowers-trapped-debt-spiral?newsfeed=true